KU-002-376

Bedtime Adventure Stories for Grown Ups

by Anna McNuff

Bedtime Adventure Stories for Grown Ups

Copyright © 2021 by Anna McNuff

All rights reserved.

No part of this book may be reproduced in any form by any electronic or mechanical means, including information storage and retrieval systems, without written permission from the author, except for the use of brief quotations in a book review.

Cover illustration by Cai Burton

@CaiBurton

joyful-design.co.uk

Book design by Sally & Kim from Off Grid

@somewhereoffgrid

somewhereoffgrid.com

If you're from a book club, corporate, business or school and would like to place a bulk order for copies of this book, substantial discounts are available.

Just drop an email to hello@annamcnuff.com for more details.

Other books by Anna McNuff:

For adults:

The Pants of Perspective

50 Shades of the USA

Llama Drama

For Kids:

100 Adventures to Have Before You Grow Up

Find Anna on Social Media:

@AnnaMcNuff

Join her mailing list:

AnnaMcNuff.com/McNewsletter

For Storm, you are my greatest adventure yet.

Contents

Your Bedtime Cup of Cocoa

Lights Out

Your Bedtime Cup of Cocoa
(Sometimes called a preface)

I never intended to write this book.

These adventures were not ones that I'd ever thought about committing to ink – they existed purely as wisps in the memory bank of my mind. Filed away, tightly held, until such a time when I would share them with my future children and grandchildren – but never more widely than that. And then, when the Covid-19 pandemic hit, everything changed. Our world was turned upside (and inside out). All of my work contracts went up in a puff of smoke and suddenly I was newly pregnant, living in a tiny flat and facing a national lockdown. Like many of us, I struggled with the loss of a sense of freedom during that time. I consoled myself by eating one too many pickled-onion sandwiches and spent the first few weeks of the pandemic being hideously unproductive.

In the UK, we went out onto the street every Thursday night to bang saucepans and clap for our National Health Service workers and, in light of their efforts to save lives, I felt useless to say the least. So (rather than eat more pickled-onion sandwiches), I asked myself what I had to 'give' to others. To

1

the online community who had supported me over many years – an army of followers who I knew loved adventure and who, like me, were feeling lost, trapped and confused. The answer? I had stories. I had oodles of them from smaller journeys completed over the years that I'd never written down.

Given that I could no longer leave my home, those stories of far-flung lands seemed more precious than ever. And perhaps, if I could help us all escape mentally, if only for an hour or so, then that might mean that we could get through the next day or the next week together. Little did I know it would actually be about getting through the next year. Cue the shocked-face emoji.

Eager to give the minds of adventurous souls a holiday from the doom of the daily news, I ran interactive bedtime storytelling sessions each week. I went live at 7.30 p.m. on Thursday for three months – answering questions from the audience before sharing a carefully selected tale of adventure each time.

Over the course of those months, thousands of wanderlusters from over 20 countries tuned in to join me on an armchair escapade. Folks in New Zealand settled down with a coffee after their morning yoga, followers in Canada sneaked off from work for mid-afternoon tea breaks to listen in and those in my own time zone ordered family-sized pizzas and labelled it ADVENTURE NIGHT. All in all, we had a blast. I did it to help others maintain their sanity through turbulent times but, in the process, I clung on to my own. The weekly sessions gave my life a rhythm. An anchor to weather the storm.

The tales in this book are the best of those shared at the live bedtime storytelling sessions. They are a mix of adventures big and small. Accounts of friendship and solitary crusades. Journeys involving fancy dress, rollerblades, bikes and kayaks. Quests over mountains, across rivers and even along the A38 in Essex. It's a pick 'n' mix bag of travel treats. Take them one at a time, dip in and dip out at random or gobble them all in one go – anything goes. However and wherever you choose to read them, my only hope is that you can find the time to snuggle up and allow yourself to be transported with me, to another time and place.

Sweet dreams,

MARATHONS AT MIDNIGHT

California.
Summer, 2018.

It's midsummer in Palm Springs, California. The sun is just beginning to set over the San Jacinto Mountains and my boyfriend Jamie and I are sitting at a cute Thai restaurant, perusing the menu. I decide to order a pad thai and take a moment to look around. The faces of fellow diners are lit by flickering candlelight, as they sit beneath windowsills covered in white orchids, lotus flowers and star-flowered jasmine. Smells of lemongrass, coconut and ginger are floating through the dining room and I feel wonderfully relaxed.

'You know what, J? I might have a glass of wine tonight,' I announce, slinking back into my chair and letting out a long sigh.

'Aww, you go for it, my dear,' he replies.

'I certainly wi… Oh no, wait.'

'What?'

'I'd better not. We've got to run a marathon after dinner…'

It was an easy thing to forget. It's not normal to begin a marathon at 10 p.m., after all. But then again, our lives were far from normal that summer. Jamie was part way through an attempt to run 6,000 miles across America, dressed as a superhero called Adventureman, and I'd flown out from the UK to spend 10 days running by his side.

In my role as supportive girlfriend, I had, of course, dressed up as Wonder Woman – opting to pair a blue and red star-spangled leotard (emblazoned with the iconic gold 'W') with navy running shorts and a red T-shirt. I was pretty sure that the leotard was actually intended for 12-year-olds, but it had come with a free gold 'lasso of truth', so that had made squeezing my grown-up 33-year-old body into it worthwhile.

Having spent a significant amount of our four-year relationship with one or the other off on an adventure, Jamie and I were used to spending large chunks of time apart, keeping the love alive through patchy phone calls and truncated text messages. But, after three months of living life independently, it had been a relief to be reunited in Palm Springs. Difficult as the distance thing was, it made our relationship exciting. I always got a kick out of the anticipation of seeing him again. I enjoyed the first few hours after a reunion, how they felt precious and strange – filled with all the butterflies and excitement you would expect from meeting a stranger on a first date, coupled with an overwhelming sense of familiarity. Despite the jitters in your belly, you know that you trust this person and that they trust you too. And you fancy the pants off them all over again.

I knew that running alongside Jamie for 10 days wouldn't be easy. I'd spent much of the flight from the UK obsessing about the many ways we could come unstuck in the arid conditions. It being mid August in southern California, temperatures during the daytime were soaring to 50°C, which meant that the only sensible thing for us to do was to run at night, when the sun was tucked up in the bed of the horizon and the air was cooler. I say sensible… Of course it wasn't sensible to be running through the desert at all at that time of year, but adventures tend to take on a life of their own and so there we were: bellies full of pad thai, on the outskirts of the city, ready to take the first few steps of our marathon through the night.

I was understandably nervous about running on unfamiliar roads at night, and Jamie was quieter than usual so I could tell that he was nervous too. But his nerves weren't anything to do with running at night. He already had plenty of experience of that and had been midnight-marathoning for the past few weeks since passing through Los Angeles. Jamie's nervousness was focussed on a knee injury he'd picked up while running into Palm Springs. In a bid to speed up our reunion and get to see me sooner, he'd decided to crack out 50 miles in a single day – damaging his knee in the process. We'd therefore dubbed those 50 miles LOVE MILES. 'Love miles are always worth it, my dear,' he'd told me earlier that afternoon. But looking at the grimace on his face as we left the restaurant, I wasn't so sure.

Pushing our collective nerves aside, we wound steadily out of town, past gay clubs blasting out trance anthems, sun-kissed California types, sipping on Mai Tais at tall tables, and palm trees adorned with fairy lights. Jamie gave a loud cheer as we swerved Caesar (Jamie's running stroller) around a couple smooching on a street corner.

'Get in there!' he hollered. The couple stopped kissing and looked at us. The man's face was smeared with red lipstick and their eyes hinted that they may have had their own glass of wine (or six) with dinner. The woman waved one arm in the air and cheered back, before resuming the street smooch-fest, and we ran on.

As the music from the bars and clubs became fainter and the city lights faded from view, we began to pass through the playground of the rich and famous. I gawped at plush country clubs, hotels, casinos and private mansions, all of them set back from the road, partially hidden behind white stone walls and tall iron gates. From then on, the hours passed in a flash. Trainers padding softly on neatly laid concrete paving slabs, we'd soon made 13 miles. We took turns to push Caesar, doing our best to extract oxygen from the hot syrup-like air and pausing every so often to stick our heads under the cool sprinklers that were watering manicured patches of roadside grass. There was a harvest moon in the sky and it looked ginormous: a lemon-yellow ball floating on the horizon, obscured every now and then by clusters of passing blue-grey cloud.

Even though it was night time, it was still 38°C and, from time to time, the humidity would really get to me. Running in that kind of heat made me feel uncomfortable in my own skin and my mouth tasted as if someone had emptied a year's worth of vacuum-cleaner dust into it. Every 5 miles or so, we'd pass a 24-hour gas station and take sanctuary in their air-conditioned convenience store – scoring a cold drink and sitting on the curb outside to gulp it down. Sparkling water for Jamie, a bottle of ice-cold chocolate milk for me.

By 2.30 a.m. on the first night of running together, we'd made 20 miles and my excitement for the task at hand had evaporated in the heat. I was exhausted. Our unquenchable thirsts were no longer being satisfied by chocolate-milk and sparkling-water stops, Jamie's knee was starting to bother him and my body craved sleep. We ran on in silence. Just two tired people shuffling along the deserted pavements, willing the finish line to come. It was close to 4 a.m when we finished that first full marathon and crawled into bed at a budget motel, 26 miles south of Palm Springs After a cold shower, we set our alarms for early the afternoon, put the air con on full blast, pulled the blackout blinds and drifted off to sleep.

After nine hours of sleep and now with less jet lag in my system, I felt refreshed – sharper and more confident as we headed out for a second night of midnight marathon action. That said, I did suspect that the neatly curved 'posh pavements' were soon to disappear. The towns were getting smaller and I knew that we would soon be running on roads with little or no shoulders on them, so I proudly pulled rank as Chief Desert Safety Officer and insisted that both of us wear high-vis vests.

'J, put this on will you…?' I said, tossing him a lightweight running vest before we began the run.

'What?! But Caesar has lights on him? People can see us.

We'll be fine,' he replied.

'I'm sure we will be fine, J-boy, but just in case we aren't, I want us lit up like Christmas trees on that road.'

'But… I look like Freddie Mercury in this!' he said, slipping the vest on over his bare chest. The look on his face was that of a disgusted teenager. I stifled a grin as I surveyed his pasty white torso, his dark chest hairs poking through the fluorescent yellow mesh of the vest. Wow. He really had channelled the spirit of Freddie in near-perfect fashion.

'I don't care. You'll be alive and you'll be safe – that's all that matters,' I said, trying not to laugh. 'And besides – you haven't got a patch on me and my… DISCO VEST!' I shouted, flicking a switch on the back of my own running vest which lit up a series of LED tubes in rainbow colours.

'Woah! That is BRIGHT.'

'Isn't it just?'

'Can you run behind me please,' he said. 'If I look at that thing for too long it's going to make me have a seizure.'

'Ah come on, J-boy, you're just jealous because I'm having my own personal party over here. Play your cards right and I might even let you turn me on. Ooo errr,' I said, flicking the light switch on the vest back and forth.

Harnessing the power of Freddie, and with the multi-coloured power of a DISCO VEST on our side, we were on our merry way by 11 p.m. Freddie – I mean, Jamie – was pushing Caesar in front and I, as requested, was running behind.

Five miles came and went with no trouble at all. By 7 miles we were storming along, having covered the distance in under 90 minutes. *With this kind of progress, we'll finish tonight's marathon in no time at all!* I thought.

At the 9-mile marker, Jamie had decided to let me run ahead and now I noticed that he was lagging behind.

'J, you alright?' I called over my shoulder, pulling Caesar to a halt. Jamie made it to where I was standing and screwed up his face. 'Not really. It's my knee. It's not good.' He sighed, rubbing his right knee cap.

As it turned out, Mr Mercury and a light-up disco vest weren't enough to ward off bad luck, and what we had hoped was going to be an easy-breezy second night of running turned into slow-motion agony as Jamie's 'love miles' knee injury flared up. We were still running, or rather, limping, when dawn broke. Just as the sun began to rise over the surrounding mountains, we accepted defeat. We'd only made 18 miles and Jamie was gutted. He still had over 3,000 miles left to run on his trans-America journey to the state of Maine, and any injury that had the potential to be an adventure showstopper was a real blow. We took refuge in the nearest motel we could find, drew the blackout blinds and crawled into bed, not knowing how long it would be before Jamie could run again.

****

We spent the following five days holed up in the city of Indio. Now, I've got nothing against Indio, it's a nice enough place – a working-class town in the Coachella Valley built on agriculture and surrounded by sand, scrub and reddish-orange peaks. But I'm not sure it'll ever be included on a list of must-visit holiday destinations and it's certainly not a place you'd want to be unexpectedly stuck for five days. Especially when the only spaces to hang out in are a small air-conditioned motel room or a fast-food restaurant. In a bid to keep my sanity while Jamie rested, I decided to shift my focus from the things I couldn't control to those that I could. That led me to thinking about the road ahead and to doing some reading about a place I hoped we'd be reaching soon – Bombay Beach, on the shores of the Salton Sea.

According to *Atlas Obscura*, the Salton Sea is a 'barren post-apocalyptic wasteland, frozen in the 1960s'. Now if that doesn't sound like a destination for a romantic couple's break, I don't know what does! Although it's called the Salton Sea, it's actually a large lake. But how on earth does a lake form in the middle of the desert, I hear you cry. I'm so glad you asked…

It all kicked off in 1905 when the Colorado River swelled and flooded a valley called the Salton Sink. The flooding continued for two years and the lake grew into a body of water 15 miles wide and 35 miles long – making it the largest lake in California. Soon, birds began to flock to the area and schools of fish thrived in 'the sea'. Property developers saw the opportunity for a unique warm-weather holiday destination within driving distance of cities on America's West Coast and dubbed the area the 'Salton Riviera'. Yacht clubs, hotels, diners and even a small town called Bombay Beach sprung up on the seashore as the area became a popular resort in the 1950s. But disaster loomed (dun dun daaa)…

Once the flooding subsided, and with no regular rainfall in the area, there was no way to maintain a flow of fresh water into the lake. Runoff water began entering the Salton Sea from nearby farms, polluting it with pesticides and making it saltier than the Pacific Ocean. 'Depleted oxygen in the sea killed fish and dragged their rotting bodies onto the beach, where they shrivelled in the sun,' says the *Obscura*. What once was a dream destination became a fishy graveyard and, as the water in the lake stagnated, so too did tourism at Bombay Beach. Each year, fewer people visited and gradually the yacht clubs, diners and hotels closed their doors and fell into disrepair. Today, the town is popular with photographers and artists who visit the shores of the sea to capture images of a derelict resort frozen in the 1950s.

Wow. What a place! I thought. There was something electric about the idea of running into a post-apocalyptic wasteland. I like anywhere in the world that's different. Better still, since we'd be running into the town of Bombay Beach about 60 years after the tourism boom, it was guaranteed to be quiet. Perfect.

By the fifth evening in Indio, Jamie's knee pain was down

to a manageable level and he was ready to hit the road. Bombay Beach was 50 miles south and we reckoned it'd take us two days to get there. To avoid the searing daytime heat, we'd lined up staying with some firefighters at a remote fire station halfway through the 50 miles, but we were struggling to find somewhere to rest our heads in Bombay Beach itself, and it was playing on my mind.

'J… I'm a bit worried we don't have anywhere to stay in Bombay Beach yet,' I said.

'Don't they have a motel or something?' he replied.

'No, it's a tiny place… 200 people, I think. There's no motel… Just one bar… called the Ski Inn.'

'Ahh, we'll just ask the firefighters – they'll know someone.'

'But what if they don't… I don't want us running out into the desert in the middle of the night with nowhere to stay when the sun comes up,' I said, biting my lip. I could swear it was my mum's voice coming out of my mouth and not my own. But I couldn't help it. If those first few days of running had showed me anything, it's that we couldn't underestimate the toll that the heat would take on our bodies. Having a cool place to stay and to get some sleep during the daytime was a necessity, not a luxury. I was all for winging it, but I wasn't up for winging it in a 50°C desert, in August.

'Okay… I'm about to go and grab some ice cubes from reception to stick in our bottles. How about I call that Bombay Beach ski bar place while I do that? I'm sure they'll know someone who can help,' he said.

Jamie headed to reception to make the phone call and came back five minutes later with a big grin on his face.

'You'll never believe this…'

'What?'

'She's from Gloucestershire.'

'Who? The receptionist?'

'No. The woman who owns the bar at Bombay Beach. Sonja – she's from Cirencester! She had a proper West Country accent and everything.'

'No way!' What were the chances that the woman running the Ski Inn, the one bar in the small town of Bombay Beach, in the middle of the Californian desert, was from our home county of Gloucestershire?

'Could she help?' I asked.

'Course she can… she says she's got a spare holiday home in town that we can have all to ourselves and stay as long as we like.' He beamed.

'Aww, how kind is that?'

'And she says she'll meet us when we arrive.'

'What… but that'll be three a.m.?!'

'Yep. I told you she was lovely. You happier now?'

Jamie asked.

'Much happier, thank you. And thank you, Sonja.'

'Shall we shake the bush then?'

'Yeah. Let's get shakin'. Bombay Beach – post-apocalyptic wasteland and home to Sonja, goddess of Gloucestershire – here we come!'

God, it felt good to be back on the road. To be moving again through the sticky heat of an August night. Even if it was 40°C and humid, to boot, I was just happy to be back out there, flushing the fast food eaten in Indio from my veins and shaking loose the uncertainty that Jamie's knee injury had dished up for our time together.

Once we got out of town, the traffic became close to non-existent. We took a series of small back roads, zigzagging our way south, following dusty tracks down the side of fields where bell peppers were growing, bulbous and red on their vines – shiny, taut skins reflecting the glare from our head torches as we shuffled on by.

Jamie's knee was holding up, and I soon discovered that I had far more energy than when we'd run out of Palm Springs. The days of enforced rest in Indio had allowed me to get over my jet lag and to acclimatise to the heat. I was now a finely honed desert warrior, or so I told myself. That illusion was shattered when a scorpion scuttled out from beneath a small shrub next to the road. Jamie screamed at the top of his lungs and I wet myself with fear. Perhaps we weren't quite desert warriors yet.

Scorpion attacks aside, it's hard to explain what it feels like to be alone as a couple in the desert at night. It seemed as if, while Jamie was recovering, the desert had held a space for us – a secret place to retreat to when the rest of the world was asleep. I revelled in the silence and simplicity of it and I began to feel greedy, having it all to ourselves.

There was a sense of reliance on one another out there too, an unspoken acknowledgement that we were a long way from a helping hand should things go tits up. And with that, the bond between us grew tighter. Sometimes we chatted as we ran; sometimes we ran in silence, listening to the sounds of nearby water sprinklers, the wind moving through leaves of date palms, the scuffle of unseen critters in the bushes, the soft patter of trainers on the earth and the turning of Caesar's wheels.

Without much to look at while we ran, I found that sight took a back seat and my other senses were heightened. I felt subtle changes in the air around us – an increase in humidity, a slight shift in the wind. The air was still hot, almost too hot to breathe, and it smelled faintly of overheated car engine. But I kind of liked that too.

Along the main highway, we ran parallel to a railway track. A freight train would pass us every hour, like clockwork – the train starting as a faint glimmer on a black horizon and transforming into a thunderous clatter of metal wheels on metal tracks as it neared. As the train whooshed past us, it carried a welcome breeze – a relief from the otherwise humid, stagnant air.

As planned, we took a day of respite at the remote fire station on the road to Bombay Beach, before continuing on- wards, towards the USA–Mexico border and this mystical place I'd now read so much about. The night we left the fire station was as magical as the one before. The stars filled the sky and, as an unexpected gift, we got to experience a full-blown meteor shower. We were an hour into that night's marathon and taking a roadside break for water when I spotted the first shooting star. They came thick and fast after that, and soon the sky looked as if someone had danced across it and left behind a trail of diamonds.

'Woah!!! J! Did you see that?!'.

'Beaawwtiful!' Jamie cooed.

I've seen hundreds of shooting stars in my lifetime, but this display was something else. The tail of one meteor was visible for a solid second as it streaked across the black sky, leaving a trail of red in its wake.

When we made it to Bombay Beach, Sonja from Cirences- ter was there waiting for us, all smiles and hugs and West Country accent – as if greeting two strangers at 3 a.m. in the car park of a bar in the middle of nowheresville was the most normal thing in the world. She led us through the dusty dark- ened streets of the town and to our bed for the night.

The next day we emerged from Sonja's air-con cocoon and spent some time exploring the town. It didn't take long to walk every inch of it. The whole town was no more than 500 metres long, with a grid of streets labelled simply A to D Street in one direction and 1st to 5th Avenue in the other. The first thing I noticed was the silence. There wasn't a soul to be seen, and wandering around, looking up and out at the mountains beyond the lake felt strangely peaceful. The majority of the houses were mobile homes with neatly maintained sandy yards but, in between, there were empty caravans with broken windows and shacks with graffiti on the walls. Burnt-out cars – Buicks, Cadillacs, Chevys and even a limousine – sat rusting on a patch of gravel at one end of town. Discarded household furniture was dotted throughout the streets and we spotted a lone, tattered armchair on the beach with its stuffing hanging out, the once bright-red upholstery heavily faded by the desert sun. Much of the town seemed fragile and forgotten. I could see why it was a popular destination for creative types – all those forgotten things had a story to tell, after all.

Sonja had insisted on treating us to brekkie at the Ski Inn, so we made our way there to fill our bellies and kill time until the temperature dropped enough for us to be able to run out of town. The inn was everything you'd hope for from the only drinking joint in a tiny town. A few locals with long white beards and even longer stories were propping up the bar, and behind them I could see a yellow sign on the wall which read: 'Nothing much happens in this town, but what you hear makes up for it.' Wooden chairs surrounded plastic-topped tables, there was a jukebox in the corner and the walls were plastered with dollar bills, which were covered in signatures –

mementos from tourists who had visited this remote outpost over the years.

With nowhere else to be and nothing else to do but rest and chat, we spent the remainder of the day at the inn, listening to Sonja reminisce about life in England (including how much she missed Bisto gravy) and talking to other residents (with and without beards) about what life was like on the shores of the Salton Sea. One man said, 'People come here looking for a different life. A quieter life.' In the brief time we'd spent in town, I could see that was true.

After thanking Sonja for her hospitality, we ran out of Bombay Beach after the moon had risen. I kept Jamie company for a few more days but soon it was time for him to continue his trans-America adventure alone. I left him just shy of the California–Arizona border and hitched a ride to a Greyhound bus station to begin my long journey home. Boarding a bus bound for Phoenix airport, I thought back on how I'd felt about this trip before leaving the UK. All that trepidation I'd had about joining Jamie to run through southern California in the middle of summer. And how something I'd been so fearful of had actually turned out to be one of the most magical experiences of my life. Quirky towns, kind people, star-filled skies and the quiet beauty of the desert. It was certainly a hot and steamy couple's retreat I'd never forget.

ROLLIN' IN ZE DAM

The Netherlands.
Spring, 2014.

When was the last time you went rollerblading? I'm going to take a punt and assume that it wasn't last week although, if that's the case, please take a moment to give yourself a giant high-five for being so darn radical. If you *have* ever rollerbladed, I'll wager that you remember it being a whole lot of fun. And if that's true, then why (oh why?) do we ever *stop* rollerblading? Was it because we grew up and became sensible? I sincerely hope not.

One spring, in an attempt to resist the dreaded threat of growing up, my friend Jo (then aged 32) and I (then aged 29) decided that we would head off on a mission to rollerblade 100 miles around Amsterdam.

I'd met Jo for the first time the previous summer through a mutual friend, and we'd hit it off immediately. She is northern, blonde and loud, with all the energy of a recently popped bottle of champagne. Her cat-like brown eyes and wry smile hint that she's always plotting something, and I got a feeling from our very first conversation that entering Jo's world meant entering a world of possibility. Jo makes her living as a presenter on various TV shows and at live festivals in the UK and abroad, and she had recently landed her dream job as the MC at the Race Village for the Volvo ocean sailing race.

It was a gig that would see her rub shoulders with the stars of the sailing world and jet set around the globe for eight months. With all that hard work ahead, Jo was eager to squeeze in one final adventure before she joined the Volvo team. So over a glass of wine in a London pub one evening, and having spent a significant chunk of time talking about how much we loved rollerblading as kids, we came up with the idea of travelling 100 miles together, on boots with wheels.

Now, 100 miles might sound like a long way to rollerblade, especially for two people who haven't been a-rollin' for some time, but 100 is such a nice round number. It sounds friendly, even. And when Jo and I asked ourselves where sounded like an equally friendly (read: flat) place to go rollerblading, the Netherlands popped into mind. So the plan was set – we would rollerblade 100 miles out and back from Amsterdam together, completing a giant loop around the Zuiderzee Bay over the space of four days.

In a bid to keep things as adventurous as possible, we decided that we'd blade with all our kit on our backs and sleep wild in bivvy bags wherever we could. As the final cherry on the adventure cake (and because the last time both of us had rollerbladed was likely in 1989), we established that we would complete the challenge dressed in 80s clothing. At least I think that was the reason. It could have been that I just love any excuse to slip into some fancy dress. Either way, one Friday morning in late spring, we each loaded a set of rollerblades, a helmet, a fluorescent orange tutu and matching leg warmers into our backpacks and headed for Amsterdam.

The trip got off to a spectacular start. British Airways had overbooked the flight from London Heathrow and so, after volunteering to move to a later flight, we were rewarded with a free breakfast and 150 euros each. The trip was supposed to cost €150 in its entirety, so the adventure had already paid for itself before we'd even left the ground. How marvellous. As an added departure bonus, our original, earlier flight was delayed and the later flight (which we'd been paid to defer to) ended up arriving in Amsterdam sooner. The adventure stars had aligned. They were shining brightly, and we were basking in their glow right from the start. Or so we thought.

Unfortunately, while we were getting suited and booted to begin the journey, our luck changed. It began to rain. We'd found an office block in the centre of Amsterdam with a partial roof and tall glass windows, which we were using as mirrors as we slipped into our 80s outfits. That's when I heard the pitter-patter of water droplets on the pavement behind us.

'Errr, Jo…'

'Yep?' she asked, adjusting her tutu and double checking that it was straight.

'It's raining.'

'Is it?' Jo spun around and saw the raindrops on the pavement too. 'So it is. Err… okay. Is rollerblading in the rain a thing?' she asked.

'I'm not sure… hang on…' I said, getting out my phone.

'What are you doing?'

'Googling it.'

'Right… of course you are,' she smiled.

I typed into the search bar: *Can you rollerblade in rain?* 'It's a thing!' I exclaimed, now reading from the screen. 'It says here that it's more difficult in the rain because the surface will be slippery, but that if you're… oh no, hang on. It says that if you're a "competent rollerblader" then it'll be fine… that's not really fine, is it?'

'Err, I don't know who you're referring to but I, for one, am darn competent,' Jo grinned, placing her hands on her hips in a Wonder Woman-style pose.

'In that case, so am I.'

With our minds now at ease about the impending weather challenge, we pulled on rain jackets over our 80s get-up and began a tentative roll over the wet pavement. I took my first few glides away from the office block and found progress to be wobbly but surprisingly smooth.

'Wahoooo! 100 miles – here we go!' I shouted, picking up confidence with every push of the blades. It was then that I realised that something was missing – Jo's voice. She was unusually quiet. 'Jo? How you getting on?' I called over my shoulder. There was no answer.

'Jo…? Jo?' I rolled to a halt and shuffled myself around to face the direction I'd come from. Jo was some 50 metres away, collapsed in a heap on the ground, laughing. What on earth was she doing? I rolled back to her.

'Sorry luv!' Jo said, throwing her arms into the air. 'I didn't make it very far!'

'What happened?'

'It's my wheels. They won't… go round.'

'What do you mean they won't go round?' I asked, thinking that this was surely the primary job of a wheel – to rotate.

'I mean, they won't move. They're stuck solid.'

She lifted a foot and poked at the four small white wheels. They didn't budge. I sat down beside her on the pavement and poked the wheels too. They were jammed solid. It was the same story on the other rollerblade boot as well.

'How did that happen? Did they seize up on the plane?' I asked, wondering if cabin pressure had some funky effect on rotating wheels. Jo hung her head.

'No… I, err… I didn't want to tell you but…'

'But?'

'I haven't actually used these rollerblades before. Ever. I borrowed them off my friend, who last used them when they were 12…' I put my head in my hands as Jo continued, now speaking more quickly and running her words together. 'I just was so nervous about this whole trip and I knew I should practise, but every time I thought about practising it made me more nervous. So I just decided to not practise at all. And here I am. Oh dear,' she wailed.

I couldn't help but laugh. I'd been nervous and done minimal practice too, but at least I had the benefit of a new pair of rollerblades, with wheels that moved. After years of gathering dust in her friend's garage, Jo's wheels were stuck fast.

'Well, they're jammed alright… maybe they're just a bit rusty though. I'm sure we can find someone with some oil or something to loosen them up. This is Amsterdam, after all – there are bike shops everywhere.'

What followed was a short waddle around the corner to the nearest bike shop and an interesting conversation with a nice Dutch man about whether he had any lube. For our wheels. Lube was applied. Motion was restored and soon we were on our way.

With Jo's wheels now doing their principal job of going round and the rain turning out to be a passing shower, we moved swiftly through the city, growing in confidence as we glided easily over the smooth red tarmac of bike lanes, and did our best to stop at road junctions. I say 'did our best' because stopping was not our forte. I was much better at the 'going' part of rollerblading than the stopping. And, with her newly lubed-up wheels, so was Jo. I had spent some time watching YouTube videos trying to learn how to stop on rollerblades but, under pressure, out there on the city streets of Amsterdam, we were forced to invent our own ways of coming to a halt. Popular examples included: clutching a nearby lamppost, running our wheels into a high curb or, as Jo so beautifully demonstrated that first afternoon, grabbing an unsuspecting passer-by. I liked to think that we were pioneers, bringing innovative ways of stopping to the rollerblading masses.

Soon the humdrum of the city began to die away and the traffic on the roads beside us got lighter as we wound our way along the shores of the Zuiderzee Bay. Lush green fields stretched towards the horizon – a sea of grass broken only by the canals, which ran inland from the bay and were lined with buttercups and daffodils. The morning rain had drenched the fields and the scent of damp earth was carried on a warm breeze. Under sunshine and blue skies, we rolled onwards, towards the town of Volendam and a place called Edam – the home of the cheese, which made me smile. It wasn't long before we were able to move away from the roadside entirely, following a network of beautifully paved canal-side trails with only curious ducks and the odd cyclist for company.

By 6 p.m. on the first evening in the Netherlands, we'd made 17 miles. It wasn't as far as we'd hoped to travel but, given the rain and Jo's lubrication issue, we decided that was fine and dandy for an adult rollerblading debut. We reasoned that we'd make up the missed miles over the following few days and celebrated with a simple dinner at a local restaurant on the water's edge, clinking our tankards of cool frothy beer as dusk fell and the now-blackened waters of the Zuiderzee began to sparkle in the moonlight.

After a night spent camped in a field not far from the shore of the bay, we were up and at 'em at dawn, winding our way down quiet backstreets and passing long rows of brownish-red terraced houses with gardens that smelled of freshly cut grass. Every now and then, a waft of morning coffee would escape from a nearby kitchen window and I'd inhale deeply, savouring the smell of a breakfast blend for just a few moments as we rolled on by.

Being springtime, the tulips were just starting to bloom – reds, yellows, purples, all swaying gently on long green stalks in front gardens. We pressed on past the tulips, loosely following the shoreline of the Zuiderzee Bay, moving towards windmills on the horizon, their large white blades turning slowly against a backdrop of pale blue and wisps of candy-floss clouds.

Saturday life in suburban Holland was in full springtime swing. Each small village that we passed through was bustling with locals either buying fresh produce from market stalls or enjoying pastries and coffee at small tables under the awning of a cafe. By mid-afternoon we were rolling through towns where the streets were cobbled instead of paved. At first that was a novelty. After what had been 35 miles of baby-smooth surfaces, the introduction of cobbles seemed like a fresh and exciting challenge. But the excitement soon wore thin as the easy gliding that we'd enjoyed over the past 24 hours was re-duced to an unglamorous hobble. If you've ever watched an ice skater step off the rink and try to walk across the carpet, that was now us. All stuck-out bums and wayward, waggling arms.

'Bloody hell, this is tough. If I'd known the ride was going to be this bumpy, I'd have double-bagged my boobs,' said Jo, clutching her chest and waddling behind me, still doing her best to roll over the cobbles on her wheels but failing miserably.

'I hear you. On the plus side, maybe this is like one of those machines that they advertise on late-night shopping channels. You know, the one that jiggles all your bits until you end up with a six-pack?'

'Well, I'll gladly take the abs, but I can do without the cobbles!' Jo replied, swinging her arms wildly back and forth in a bid to speed up her cobble-hobble.

Cobbles aside, the second day of our adventure was everything that I'd hoped a rollerblading journey would be. With the wind blowing on my face and the sun warming my cheeks, I felt as free as a bird. We were moving across the Dutch landscape faster than if we had been walking and with far less effort than it would have taken to run. All in all, I wondered whether perhaps rollerblading was the ultimate way to travel? And that led me to start daydreaming about what adventures I might like to do in the future, ones that involved rollerblading further than a friendly sounding 100 miles…

My daydreaming was interrupted by a new feature on the horizon – a small, curved bridge over a canal. It was a cute wee thing with a metal railing on each side and, as I approached it, I wondered how best to get up and over safely. I made a split-second decision and concluded that I just needed to go for it. So, without saying anything to Jo who was behind me, I put in a few extra-hard glides and whooshed up and over the hump of the bridge, before bringing myself to a jerky stop (by clutching a lamppost) on the other side.

I turned around to look for Jo. She'd gotten halfway across the bridge and was now standing in the middle of it. She'd adopted some kind of awkward squat position and was clinging on to the metal railings.

'How did you do it?' she called, scanning the ground and looking for the best route down the other side.

'Err, I just went for it. I think that's the best way,' I shouted back.

'Just go for it?' she asked.

'Yeah! But don't try to stop yourself, you've really got to—'

But it was too late. Jo was already three glides deep into her own version of 'going for it'. She made it halfway towards me before her brain must have screamed at her that 'going for it' was a truly terrible idea, and she faltered. I watched, almost in slow motion, as Jo spun her arms wildly like a Dutch windmill. At first, I thought she was going to fall backwards and land on her bum but, at the last minute and at the steepest point of the bridge, she threw her body forwards, stretched her arms out and fell forwards onto her hands. Her palms were pressed firmly into the ground and there they stayed as her body kept moving over the top of them. I watched as the fingers and wrist on her right hand bent in a direction that no fingers and wrist ever should and there was a loud craaaaack! And then... silence.

Oh god, I knew it was bad. I mean, it sounded bad. I

rushed over to where Jo was sitting on the ground, clutching her right hand. 'Oh my gosh, Jo! Are you okay?' I said, already overcome with guilt about telling her to 'just go for it'.

'I'm fine. Well… crikey… that hurt! Okay, I'm not fine… just gimme a minute… I'll be okay in a minute,' she said, letting out a long breath. And I knew that she was already showing signs of shock.

Jo took a few more deep breaths and continued to sit on the road in silence, shutting her eyes whenever a wave of pain hit. I sat next to her, not knowing what to do or say. We didn't know one another that well after all, not well enough for me to gauge how she might react to an accident. This was supposed to be a jolly little adventure together, not a bone-bending masterclass in roadside injury management. Jo exhaled loudly again.

'Okay. I can carry on. Just let me have a sit down and a bit more rest and then I can get back up and carry on rollerblading.' I couldn't believe my ears, but I knew it was the shock talking.

'Jo… I hate to break it to you, but I don't think you can get back on those blades,' I said softly.

'No, I am. I will. It'll be absolutely fine,' she said quickly. 'It's just a bruise. I mean, my hand, it's bruised – that's all.'

'Okay… it's your call…'

'I just need a cup of tea and a sit down or something. Is there somewhere we can get a cuppa nearby?' she asked.

I checked the map. The next town was 4 miles further on. I asked Jo whether she thought she could walk that far and she said that she could, so, after getting her out of her rollerblades, we got her trainers out of her backpack and eased her feet into them. I put on my trainers too and, with the rollerblades strapped onto our backs, we set off on a 4-mile walk to town.

In town, we found a cafe with tables outside in the sunshine and, over a good old-fashioned cup of tea, we called an emergency adventure meeting. By this point, Jo's right hand had really started to swell. She decided that it now looked the size of a baby elephant and so we began to refer to it as 'ELEPHANT HAND' (always said in that *X Factor*-style voice). We discussed the idea of going to a nearby hospital, but Jo said that she didn't want to 'waste time' sitting in Accident and Emergency. I wanted to push her to get her hand looked at, but at the end of the day, she was a grown woman and it was her decision. 'Oh, Anna. I'm so sorry for ruining our adventure,' said Jo, looking down at her tea and fiddling with the teabag. *Did she actually say that?!* I thought. *This woman is mad!*

'Jo. This is an adventure. Things like this happen on adventures. In fact, it probably wouldn't be an adventure if things like this didn't happen. Yes, we were trying to rollerblade 100 miles around Amsterdam. But now we're not. Instead we'll sit here for a bit longer, we'll drink this tea and we'll work out what our new adventure looks like. Deal?' I said.

'Deal,' Jo smiled.

Instead of a hospital visit, Jo settled for me buying her a

stash of ibuprofen from a nearby pharmacy. More importantly, I also bought two Magnum ice creams. However, Jo wasn't
feeling up to eating hers so I took one for the team and inhaled
both of them, licking the wooden lolly sticks clean so that we
could use those to splint her bruised fingers, to try to keep
them straight. After fastening the ice-cream splints in place
with some tape, I completed our first-aid mission by fashioning
Jo's 80s leg warmers into a sling for her hand.

Over another cup of tea, we made a new plan for our
Rollin' in Ze Dam adventure. We would continue the 100-mile
loop around the Zuiderzee, but we'd walk rather than roll the
rest of the way. So, with Jo now adorned with two Magnum
sticks to hold her fingers straight and a fluorescent-orange
leg-warmer sling, we set off from town. We were, of course,
still wearing our 80s tutus. That was purely for medicinal pur-
poses too.

Over the following 12 hours, Jo's ELEPHANT HAND
continued to grow in size and turned some spectacular shades
of purple and blue. Soon we settled into a new teamwork
routine and came up with strategies to ease her suffering. Jo
couldn't get her backpack off, nor could she pull down her
trousers by herself, so whenever she needed to go for a wee,
I was appointed chief de-robing officer. After a wild wee in
the bushes, we often ended up in fits of giggles as a result of
me accidentally shoving Jo over while trying to help her pull
up her trousers. It was a mistake that resulted in an impressive tangle of arms, trousers, rollerblades, backpacks and the
ELEPHANT HAND. Quite the treat for any passers-by.

With the world now moving by at a slower pace and with us not having to concentrate on whether we were about to fall over every 10 minutes, our minds were freer for deeper conversations. We talked about life, love, and our hopes for the future. No small talk, just the really important things. We talked about how Jo's new bosses at the Volvo Ocean Race might take the news about her hand and how she would cope if they decided to hire someone else in her place.

Not only did Jo insist on carrying on with the adventure on foot as best we could, she also insisted on still sleeping wild in bivvy bags. I have a picture of her from the night after her accident, brandishing her ELEPHANT HAND at the camera, grinning like a goon (presumably delirious with exhaustion and pain), but with her sleeping mat laid out in front of her, and seemingly very chuffed with herself.

****

Jo and I never did make it the full 100 miles around the Zuiderzee Bay. After a mixture of rollerblading and walking 75 miles in total, we reached the brink of exhaustion and decided to call it quits, opting to board a bus to the city for the remaining 25 miles and face-plant into a fully loaded Dutch pancake, before catching our flight home.

ANNA MCNUFF

Soon after returning to the UK, Jo did the sensible, grown-up thing and went to the hospital to get her hand checked out. It was broken in two places and the doctors promptly put it in a cast, which they said was to stay on for eight weeks. I was shocked to hear that the cast wasn't made primarily from ice-cream sticks, but it was perfectly shaped for her to be able to hold a microphone in it. So Jo was able to keep her job as the MC for the Volvo Ocean Race and, given that the race's motto was 'Life on the edge', her boss recognised that a broken hand, resulting from an attempt to rollerblade 100 miles around Amsterdam, was living proof of that.

All in all, our rollerblading adventure was a complete disaster – but only in the sense that it ended up vastly different from what we had planned. And I'm grateful for that. Because in all the time we spend making plans, we never stop to question whether things going as expected is actually what matters most. Truth be told, Jo and I are better friends today because we *couldn't* rollerblade 100 miles. It's only when things fall apart that you begin to see the true measure of a friend, after all. You'll find out whether they're the type of person who will insist on sleeping in bushes with a broken hand because they don't want to let the side down, and whether they'll fashion you a sling from an 80s legwarmer and pull your trousers up after you've been for a wee. In short, instead of learning what a person can do, you learn who they are. And in place of things always going to plan, I'll take laughs, some deep conversation, a few broken bones and endless cups of emergency tea any day.

BEYOND MY BACK GATE

Europe.
Winter, 2016.

It's early morning on the shores of the Rhine River in West Germany and the sun is beginning to rise. Fingers of golden light reach across the water, touching frosted branches on steep, forest-covered hills on the opposite bank. Beside me, the grey-blue waters are flowing strongly down the valley, silent and mighty, on a section of the river that's half a mile across.

The riverside bike path ahead of me is quiet and I'm enjoying easy pedal-progress on its smooth tarmac – revelling in the rush of blood to my legs and the cool winter air whipping at my cheeks. There are a few walkers here and there along the path. I smile as I pass but they're gone in a flash. Just then, I spot something which causes me to bring my bike to a stop – a castle, perched like an angel on top of a Christmas tree close to the peak of a hill on the opposite bank. It's made from cream-coloured stone which glows amber in the dawn light and looks like something from a Disney movie.

I prop my bike against a stone wall at the river's edge and sit on a nearby bench to stare at the castle, gathering my thoughts for the day ahead. Beyond the calm and quiet of a sunrise bike ride, the best and worst thing about today is that I have no idea what it will bring. And I don't mean that in a wistful, romantic sense. I actually, truly have no idea. I don't know where I'll be sleeping tonight, what town or even what country I might wake up in tomorrow. I don't know whom I might meet or who might help me along the way. It is intoxicating and suffocating all at once. It's an adventure unlike any other.

****

When it comes to thinking about the future, there are two kinds of people in the world: planners and 'fly by the seat of their pant-ers'. Of course, it's not always so black and white, and most people sit somewhere on the spectrum between the two, but I'd love you to consider, for a moment, which you are. Do you like to think ahead and form some kind of image in your mind about how things might pan out? Or are you a 'roll with it' kind of person, someone who wakes up each morning and goes with the flow?

I am a planner. Or rather, I am 70% planner, 30% roll with it. I'm acutely aware that the complete absence of a plan makes me uncomfortable. I'd go so far as to say that having no plan at all makes me feel wriggly in my own skin. Unsettled, anxious even. I get especially frustrated when important plans change suddenly or, more specifically, when something I've been looking forward to for days, months or years suddenly disappears from view. I need time to adjust when that happens. And yet, I still love to plan.

Over the past decade I've planned and headed off on a number of adventures that have pushed me physically – running and cycling long distances for months on end. But in the February of 2016, I decided that it was time for me to try something different. Instead of exploring what made me physically uncomfortable, I wondered what it might be like to do an adventure that was guaranteed to make me mentally uncomfortable. An adventure where I couldn't plan at all. So I decided that I would set aside a month in my diary and set out on a journey into the unknown from the back garden of my London home, armed with nothing more than a bivvy, a backpack and a devil-may-care attitude. And I would let the good people of social media tell me where to go. Every few days I would post a voting option for the general public – which effectively boiled down to turn left, turn right or keep going straight on. Whichever direction the majority decided upon, that's where I'd head. When the finish line gong sounded in the middle of March – wherever in the world I found myself, whatever I was doing – I'd catch a flight home. Simples. I got down with the kids and created hashtags so that people could easily follow the journey, and I even came up with a name for the adventure: 'Beyond My Back Gate'. Because, beyond our back gate is the world and it's a crying shame not to explore it at every opportunity.

Despite the lack of a plan, I did set a few parameters for the trip – rules of engagement if you will. These included things like: big flights were out but ferries were in (both for environmental and financial reasons). The journey would need to be majority human-powered, although I was open to hitching rides from time to time. And, most importantly, I let the public know that if I ended up somewhere where there was a camel, they'd best believe that I'd be riding that noble beast as far as I could.

As if heading off on a new adventure wasn't enough, I also decided to use the end of the trip as an opportunity to make a fresh start by moving to the West Country to be with my boyfriend, Jamie. In for a penny as they say… I was going to pack all my possessions into boxes, leave the UK as a Londoner and return as a fully-fledged country bumpkin.

Despite my belief that the move west was a step in the right direction and that 'Beyond My Back Gate' was one of my better adventure ideas, when departure day arrived, my mind was a jumbled mess. There was a large part of me that wanted to shut my eyes, curl up in a ball and pretend I hadn't gone and told everyone that I was going to do this trip – or move across the country afterwards. Because, quite frankly, my London life was lovely. It's a life that I clung to like a snuggly blanket. I woke up each morning with a decent idea of how the day would pan out. I knew where my favourite coffee shop was. I knew how long it took to get from the flat I was renting in Brixton to Victoria Station on the tube. I knew where I'd sleep at night and that I wouldn't have to resort to awkward sign language and smiles to have a conversation with someone who didn't speak my language. The thought of leaving all of that behind made me feel uncomfortable. But that was precisely the point. And I resolved that I would learn a whole lot more about the world, and myself, by moving towards that discomfort rather than away from it.

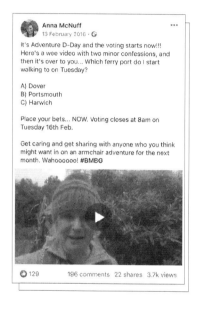

In a bid to distract myself from pre-departure nerves, I marked the start of the journey by inviting five friends for breakfast at the flat. Some of them I knew well, others I'd met only briefly, but each of them had agreed to join me for as much of the first day of the adventure as they could. Between mouthfuls of muesli and slurps of orange juice, the six of us ceremoniously counted the votes from the first post. In a toss-up between three UK ferry ports, the general public had decided that they'd like to see me stroll to Harwich on the east coast of England. There's only one ferry route out of Harwich so the vote result meant that I'd be bound for the Netherlands.

At 11 a.m. we clambered over the fence in my Brixton back garden – because I didn't actually have a back gate and it seemed more exciting than leaving via the front door. We dropped down into the local park and the mini merry rabble of five fellow adventurers and I began the walk to Harwich, some 120 miles away. It was a cold February morning so we took our sweet time, stopping often for coffee breaks in small cafes and even detouring to a large sporting-goods store in East London to collect a few things – like a spork – that I'd neglected to pack. You can't go anywhere in life without a spork, after all.

I was still a bundle of nerves on that first day, caught in the strange space between leaving familiarity and knowing it would be a long time before I found my way back to it. Every now and then, mostly when I felt tired, I would start wondering whether this was a silly idea – the walking, the adventure, the moving to a different part of the UK, all of it. I'd quickly pull back from those thoughts, doing my best to distract myself by chatting to the rest of the group. If I could just ignore the worry, then perhaps it would disappear.

We meandered through London, leaving its skyscrapers and smog behind as we moved into the sprawling suburbs, and then spent the first night camping on a patch of scrubland on the outskirts of Brentwood, Essex. On the second day of the journey, friends came and went – many of them had lives, homes and jobs to get back to, after all. I packed each of them off with a hug and a hearty thank you and welcomed the new friends who joined in for a few miles, bringing fresh blood and novel chit-chat to an increasingly subdued bunch of weary walkers.

When dusk fell on day two, I'd walked 57 miles and the excitement of getting the adventure underway had worn thin. My feet ached, my shoulders hurt, my backpack was beginning to cut into my hips and my head felt heavy. I met my friend Simon in the car park of a local fish and chip shop near Colchester and, after a wholesome dinner of fish and chips avec extra saveloy sausage, he transported me to his home to stay for the night. I had a brief chat with Simon's wife and kids, who said what I was doing was 'sick' (which I believe is a good thing), before heading upstairs for a shower.

Now alone for the first time since leaving Brixton, I had time to check in with my body and, also, to take stock of how my mind was doing. I opted to deal with the body first and inspected my blistered feet. Yikes. They were in worse shape than I'd thought. The balls of them were red raw and there was a giant beast of a bulge between my first and second toes on each foot. I took care not to tear the skin as I peeled back the tape and plasters that I'd put over the worst-affected areas, and assumed a starfish position on my back, on the bathroom floor. I let out a deep sigh and stared at the ceiling. Jeez, I was tired. And then it hit me. A wave of emotion thundered onto the shore of my mind like a tsunami. It carried with it all of the thoughts that I'd been trying to push aside for two days. *What the heck was I doing?! My feet were in bits! How was I going to carry on walking tomorrow? I didn't want to do a month of this!* I was exhausted. My feet hurt. My brain hurt. Everything hurt. Worse than that…everyone was watching and waiting for my next move. What had I got myself into? I was an idiot. It was all too much.

Tears rolled down my cheeks onto the cold, cream lino floor. I got up to run the shower to drown out the sound of my sniffs. If Simon's family, downstairs in their living room, heard me having a cry, they'd wonder who on earth they'd let into their home. I knew that walking for hours each day with no set destination would take some getting used to, but I also had a feeling that the tears were about more than just the state of my feet…

THE MELTDOWN

I'd wanted to leave London for a while and move to the West Country. What I haven't mentioned is that I'd gone one step further to move my life in a new direction. Not only had I packed up my flat for good and told friends and family that I was moving to Gloucester, I'd also handed in my notice at my marketing job. I'd hoped to spend the month on the road in quiet contemplation, to allow space for creative ideas to flow freely and to return home to the UK with a renewed sense of purpose and clarity about what to do next. So, when I clambered over my back fence in Brixton that first day, I wasn't just leaving the UK for a month. I was leaving the entirety of my old life behind, for good.

Until starfishing on the bathroom floor in Simon's house, my mind had been consumed with preparation for *this* journey. But, now that I'd started it, there was space for my thoughts to run wild. Given that my brain is a living, breathing funfair on an average day, with this added freedom it became a full-blown Six Flags Magic Mountain Amusement Park. Everything felt completely topsy-turvy.

I continued to stare at the ceiling as steam from the hot shower filled the bathroom and realised I'd never actually started a journey from my own front door before. In the past, on longer adventures, I'd hopped on a plane and cannon-balled right into the adventure-action. I now realised that the cannonball approach was an easier way to begin. Taking a plane to the start point of a journey is like ripping off a plaster at high speed. Starting from your front door is a slow peel, one of those agonising removals that catches every hair and raw flap of skin along the way. Walking away from home was mentally painful. Worse still, the instability of not knowing where I was going physically on this adventure had now collided with having no idea of where I was going metaphorically in life. I couldn't visualise what my days would be like for the month that lay ahead, nor could I grasp what they looked like beyond that. I felt out of control, like a car with no handbrake rolling downhill.

Hauling myself up from the floor, I wiped away my tears and, feeling guilty about running up Simon's water bill, I got into the shower at last. I winced as soapy water ran over the cuts left by the backpack on my hips, making them sting, and continued to contemplate my options. Pulling my thoughts back from the impending black hole of life-doom that I was rapidly being sucked into, I tried to focus on the immediate problem. Which I decided was: the walking. Walking was crap. Not only was it painful for my bod, it was painfully slow for my mind too. Where in the name of Mary and Moses did I get the idea that walking for a month might be fun in the first place? Sure, strolling to the nearest UK ferry port had had all the ingredients for success – the company of friends, relaxed chats, pub dinners and sleeping wild in woods. But with less control over my route, it was far from the carefree, hilltop wandering that I'd envisioned. As it turned out, walking down the side of dual carriageways through London and Essex is about as much fun as stuffing chilli into your eyeballs.

I knew that something had to give. I had to try something, anything, different to get myself out of this adventuresome pickle. By the time I'd gotten out of the shower, put on clean clothes and moved into the bedroom, I knew what I had to do. There was only one man I needed to call. A friend who was always there to get me out of a fix. I picked up my phone and I hit dial…

'Stace?'

'Hello McNuff, this is a bit late for you to be calling isn't it. What's up?'

'Yeah, it's getting close to my bedtime. Am I disturbing you?'

'Not at all, mate. Go ahead.'

'Well… you know you said that I should give you a call if I needed anything?'

'Yup. Fire away.'

'Do you reckon you could get my bike for me?'

'Your bike? I thought you were walking…?' he said.

'I am… I mean, I have been. It's just. I hate it. It's crap. My feet are cut to ribbons and the pace is so slow. I'm going to go insane. I think if I get on the bike, then I'll feel better… I might be able to cope.'

Stace laughed. 'I don't blame you. I could have told you that walking was rubbish. I do have a motorbike you know… you could borrow that?' he jibed.

'Nah – you're alright – I like the pedalling. I'll stick with a pushbike. Can you come and meet me in Colchester tomorrow though? I'm off to Harwich, so it'll be a short pedal to the ferry from there.'

'Right you are, McNuff. I'll bring the dogs too. They'd love to say hello.'

'You're an angel, my friend. Super Stace to the rescue.'

'Always a pleasure.'

I hung up the phone, flopped backwards on the bed and breathed a sigh of relief. A huge weight had lifted. I knew that if I carried on walking, I was signing myself up for a month of misery. I was pleased that I hadn't given up on the idea of the unplanned adventure altogether, but changing the method of travel felt embarrassing to say the least. It would take some explaining to those already invested in and following the journey, but I'm a big believer that it's never too late to take a detour from the pathway you once chose in good faith. In short, if you don't like something, change it.

Anna McNuff
February 19, 2016

VOTING POST: This knight in shining armour (named Stace) has delivered beautiful Boudica the bicycle into my loving arms!! I'll be back on track shortly, gunning it along the roads and onto the ferry at Harwich tonight. Now, here's the question: When I get off of the ferry at the Hook of Holland at 8am tomorrow morning, where do I head?

A) Down into Belgium for waffles and beer

B) To visit a friend in Utrecht (Holland) for homely hugs and Dutch pancakes

C) Into Germany for Currywurst and Apfelstrudel

This vote closes at 9am on Saturday 20th Feb. GO! GO! GO!

PASS THE DUTCHIE

True to his word, Super Stace arrived in Colchester with the bike the following day and, after a round of face-licking from his dogs, I was on the road again, heading for the ferry at Harwich with the wind in my hair. To be moving at *such* speed (read 10 mph) felt liberating. Any reservations I'd had about switching modes of transport were left behind, squashed into the tarmac on the backroads of Essex, beneath the spinning of legs and the whir of wheels.

By 9 p.m., I'd wheeled my bike onto the Stena Line overnight ferry from Harwich and was bound for Hook of Holland. In contrast to the drama of the previous 24 hours, the journey across the North Sea was a civilised affair. I boarded in darkness, ordered dinner at the on-board cafe, drank a beer, called Jamie and retreated to my cosy cabin for eight hours of sleep. In the morning, at 6.30 a.m., Bobby McFerrin's 'Don't Worry, Be Happy,' played over the ship's tannoy, gently roused me from my slumber and let me know I had an hour to disembark.

Thanks to Bobby's reggae vibes I rolled onto Dutchie soil feeling fresh as a daisy. The clunky start to the journey was well and truly behind me and I was ready to greet the Netherlands with open arms. A fresh set of votes had been cast overnight and, as instructed, I began riding towards Rotterdam, revelling in the neat, well-surfaced bike paths along the way. I was amazed at how much calmer the experience of cycling is when separated entirely from the cars and trucks on the road. The only peril I faced on the bike paths in Holland was missing the signposted turn-off for my particular bike route. Nightmare.

I rode on, wheeling by quaint, quirky egg-shaped homes–painted white with green shutters and red trim around the doors. I passed bike racks, in the woods, made from fallen tree logs and pedalled by more people on bicycles than I could count. I stopped many times to eat thick Dutch pancakes the size of my torso and was permitted by the voters to visit some friends in the city of Utrecht. It was an odd thing to message those friends and let them know I *might* be coming to see them for the first time in five years, but only if the general public allowed it. They thought I was mad but welcomed me with open arms anyway.

Every day or two, I'd check the map for the towns or cities that were roughly 60–100 miles from where I was at the time. I'd then select three of those places, post them as options and a new vote was cast. Despite a small group of scallywag followers doing their best to send me north towards Scandinavia (in winter), the majority showed more compassion and continued to direct me east across the Netherlands, where my appreciation for the people who live there went from strength to strength. After receiving a message from a talented artist who insisted that she wanted to paint my portrait and feed me Dutch liquorice, I backtracked from Utrecht to the small town of Woerden to take her up on her offer of a sweet treat and a bed for the night. The following afternoon, she painted my picture as promised – making me look regal on a canvas

– and we spent the evening drinking beer together and eating Bitterballen. Who knew deep-fried creamed meat could taste so good?!

Anna McNuff
Published by Princess McNuff · February 21, 2016 · 🌐

Way back before the first vote had even been cast, a lady named Margo commented on the Book of Face, saying that I should visit for cheese and liquorice. As it turns out she only lives 10 miles from Utrecht. So I thought it was only right that I ride back to say hello. Of course, she's a total gem. Plus, she's introduced me to beer and Bitterballen. Double gem.

When I leave Margo's in the morning I'll be wheeling my way to... Wait for it... APELDOORN!! It's clear that you I... **See More**

After Woerden, I headed towards Apeldoorn in the hope of meeting a group of monkeys that lived in a palace there. Sadly, the monkeys were tucked away for the season (I suspect they'd actually gone on holiday), so I settled for a pedal through the forest surrounding the town and spent the night in the home of a local teacher whose cheery spirit more than made up for the lack of monkeys.

Soon, the votes began to direct me south towards Nijmegen, just shy of the German border. There, I had my first-ever longboarding lesson with Jesse – a student who had once longboarded all the way to Copenhagen in Denmark. He'd been watching my journey unfold online and reached out to offer me a place to stay in town. Jesse was determined that, even though he was 10 years my junior, he would make me as cool as him and his student friends. He failed, but I enjoyed the attempt nonetheless. We went out for pizza and I listened to Jesse talk passionately about volunteering at the refugee camp that had been set up on the outskirts of the city. He was brimming with hope for the future but, perhaps wisely, he had more faith in his own ability to create change in the world than in any government's, he said. I later met Jesse's girlfriend and I spent the night sleeping on the floor of his dorm room, with the two of them in the bed 6 ft away. They promised me that they would hold off gettin' jiggy that night, but I put my ear plugs in just in case.

The following morning, Jesse joined me for a ride out of the city. We pedalled along quiet backroads in light snowfall and he continued to talk about all his grand post-graduation plans. He wanted to travel, to continue his own adventures and to do some good in the process. His youthful exuberance and willingness to challenge those in positions of power made me wish I'd had more courage, when I was younger, to do the same. We parted ways at a cafe just over the German border.

'Well, good luck changing the world, Jesse,' I said as we hugged goodbye.

'And good luck to you too, Anna. I'll be following along,' he smiled.

Stocked up on good vibes from friendly strangers, I was well and truly into the adventure groove by the time I was a few days' ride into Germany. Keeping tabs on the voting was intense, to say the least, and the complete absence of any ability to make plans was still proving a challenge, but the journey was also turning out to be more fun than I'd imagined.

My own enjoyment wasn't the only thing about the trip that was taking me by surprise: I was blown away by how invested those following the journey online had become. Each voting post was greeted with a flood of responses as followers shared images of their own visits to the towns and villages that I was passing through. I could see that they were swept up in a tornado of nostalgia, finding comfort and joy in fond memories from years gone by. I realised that this was turning out to be a Russian doll of journeys – with dozens of other adventure stories being neatly slotted into the one I was living through.

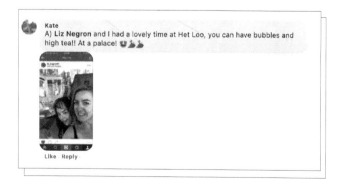

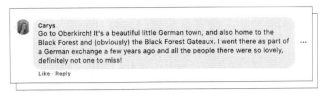

Carys
Go to Oberkirch! It's a beautiful little German town, and also home to the Black Forest and (obviously) the Black Forest Gateaux. I went there as part of a German exchange a few years ago and all the people there were so lovely, definitely not one to miss!

Like · Reply

Bill
Definitely "C"! There is so much history along the Rhone Valley as well as beautiful scenery and excellent wine. I did a river cruise on the Rhone a couple of years ago, I consider it the most senic area of France, aND Lyon is my favourite French city. Did I mention excellent wine? (I'm surprised you know "Dad's Army)

Like · Reply ·

Of course, nothing lasts forever, good or bad, and a few days after crossing the border into Germany, I faced a new challenge. The language barrier. I love language – words are one of my favourite things in the world, but my grasp of them in anything beyond English leaves a lot to be desired. Confident as I am talking to anyone and everyone in English, I'd forgotten just how nervous I get when trying to speak other languages. In my mind, all of my secondary school GCSE linguistics skills are always there, just beyond my reach. Then again, considering that I had once announced in a French exam that I *was* a hamster, instead of that I *had* one as a pet, perhaps my GCSE skills didn't count for much anyway. Funnily enough, I have no problem speaking the lingo when I'm drunk or talking to small children (not at the same time), but if I'm sober and talking to adults, whatever the foreign language,

I get embarrassed and clam up.

One morning, I spent 20 minutes desperately wanting to order a cheese and ham sandwich and a second cup of coffee in a German bakery, but failed to pluck up the courage to ask. The assistant behind the counter had struggled to understand my attempt at German while I was ordering the first cup, and that had led to excessive mumbling and the use of hand signals. Even the thought of another confused look on her face was making me wriggle in my skin, so I concluded that any further attempts to order would end up being so awkward that I'd want to climb into the oversized dough mixer behind her.

The language battle in the bakery wasn't an isolated incident. Since leaving the Netherlands (where almost everyone I'd met spoke English) I had mumbled and stumbled my way through many everyday adventure tasks such as asking for directions, buying inner tubes in a bike shop and requesting a water-bottle refill. In light of the fact that I was pedalling solo, across a continent, reliant on the help of strangers, the struggle to find words and the courage to utter them might seem ridiculous, but that didn't change the fact that *I* struggled with it. And yet it was while sitting in that bakery – feeling hungry, frustrated and wholly unsatisfied – that I realised that this was precisely what I'd left home in search of. I'd come on this journey to explore the edges of myself, after all. Because, really, the edges of ourselves are the parts that are worth getting to know better. We know the middle parts of our minds well. Those middle bits are where we're comfortable and spend most of our time. But the squiffy edges, they often get forgotten. And there's hidden treasure to be discovered there.

After just two weeks of not being able to plan, of attempting to speak foreign languages and of all-in-all hanging out with the uncomfortable parts of my character, I'd learnt that I would honestly rather run up a mountain naked, carrying a 30-kg backpack, or give a talk to a room full of 3,000 people than I would order a cheese and ham sandwich in German. Now what on earth is that about? I wasn't sure, but it really was very annoying. So, I made a vow to keep testing my terrible German on waitstaff, bike shop owners and unsuspecting shopkeepers until it ceased to feel so awkward.

I managed to pluck up the courage to order enough food and drink to keep me well-fuelled over the days that followed and, by the time I made it to the shore of the Rhine, I was averaging 60–70 miles a day and had condensed my 'planning' into neat one or two-day cycles. So long as the votes came in and I had at least a few hours to get my head around where I was headed next, I felt comfortable. What's more, I wasn't having to roll out my camping mat nearly as often as I'd expected. As it turned out, there are a lot of friends of friends, or members of the European adventure community, who will welcome a smelly cycle tourist into their homes at a moment's notice. Many of them said that they actually preferred that I had arrived at their door with such short notice because they themselves didn't know what they'd be up to the following week, or even the next day.

After whizzing through the cities of Duisburg and Dusseldorf, I passed many Disney-esque castles perched high on the hills around the cobbled riverside towns of Bonn and Koblenz. In Koblenz, I sat on a bench at sunrise and watched the morning mist rising from the river and creeping towards one of the castles. Then, after 700 miles of pedalling, I left the shores of the Rhine and headed towards a place that I'd heard much about and was very excited to visit – the Black Forest.

The Black Forest is a tree-covered mountain range in southern Germany peppered with swift-flowing rivers and alpine lakes. Phwoooar! Even saying its name, "Schwarzwald", gets my adventure juices flowing. It had always sounded like a mythical land to me, somewhere more likely to be found in *The Lord of the Rings* than on any adventure of mine. It's also the inspiration for one of the greatest 80s desserts ever invented – the Black Forest gateau. I'm not sure if the gateau was actually invented in the 80s, but that's certainly when I started eating it, or rather stealing slices during from my parents' dinner parties.

After a week of trucking along a straight, flat, paved trail beside the Rhine, I was sorry to leave the riverside cities and castles behind, but with one flick of the navigational wrist, I took a turning off the main road and was transported to another world.

In the shadow of the Black Forest evergreens, the temperature dropped. I could see my breath on the air and the change in scenery was immediate. Gone were the greys and blues of the riverside world I'd just left – in the forest everything was green, brown or reddish orange. I was surrounded by towering pine trees, with tall, slim trunks shooting skyward and green-clad branches swaying in the breeze. It reminded me of the Redwood Forests in California. Although the trees in the Black Forest were far smaller, the feeling of being surrounded by giants of nature was the same. I pedalled on, following rough rubble trails, passing over roots and rocks, climbing steadily, working my way deeper into the mystery of the mountains. I was headed for the home of a local lady who spoke English and had kindly offered (via social media) to host me for the night.

Maria lived in a small village in the forest, just above the treeline. When I rolled into the village, it was beginning to get dark and the roofs of the houses were dusted with snow, slick grey tiles sparkling in the last rays of sunlight. When I turned into Maria's driveway, she was waiting for me in the doorway of her home.

'Anna!' she said, throwing her arms open wide.

'Maria!' I replied, hopping of my bike and going over for a hug.

'Come… you must be cold… put your bike in the garage and come inside.'

After safely stowing my bike, I made my way up the stairs and into Maria's kitchen. She invited me to take a seat at her breakfast bar and went into whirlwind host mode.

'Okay – what can we get you to drink? Coffee? Tea? Hot chocolate? Wine… beer?' she smiled.

'Ohhh, something hot would be lovely, please,' I said, wiggling my toes and willing them to come back to life. 'Tea, please,' I continued.

'OK! Tea it is. And I have a surprise for you,' said Maria as she laid a fork down on the counter.

'A surprise for me?'

'Yes. Well, you are in the Black Forest now. And I know that you have been talking about Black Forest gateau in your voting posts…'

'Ah, yes… I have…' I smiled, looking down – now embarrassed that I had been banging on about it so publicly, and how I was going on a mission to find myself a slice of it before I left the forest. It was probably all a little cliché for a local.

'Well…' said Maria, moving over to the fridge. 'I had to queue for two hours in the bakery, because it is very popular, but… here you go!' She slid a box on the table and opened up the lid. Inside were two gigantic wodges of creamy, gooey Black Forest gateau. Each slice was the size of my head, with

juicy kirsch-soaked cherries poking out of it, and I began salivating.

'No way! Thanks so much. That looks amazing!'

'Let's hope it is amazing. Go on… eat!' she said.

'Great…!' I said, loading up the fork and taking a big mouthful of sponge.

'Good?' Maria asked.

'So good!' I said, trying not to spit pieces of cake onto the breakfast bar. I swallowed the first mouthful and then noticed that Maria hadn't started hers.

'Do you want me to get you a fork?' I asked, now realising that she'd only laid one out on the breakfast bar and how rude it was of me to take it.

'Oh, no. I don't like cake. I bought two pieces for you. You must be very hungry since you have cycled from London to south Germany. And with all that worry of not knowing where you are going, too,' she winked. 'That uses up calories! So, you can eat. We can chat. Maybe we can have some wine and then, later, I will make dinner and we can eat some more?' she smiled.

Blimey. Eating both slices was going to be a challenge, but I was up for it. Fork in hand, I loaded up another mighty mouthful and (while preparing my stomach for the onslaught of cream, sponge and cherry) considered the journey ahead. Despite the rocky start, my meltdown, struggles with languages and the general levels of discomfort, perhaps this unplanned adventure idea was going to work out after all…

Anna McNuff is in **Marxzell**.
February 29, 2016 · 🌐

I AM IN THE BLACK FOREST!!! Lovely host Maria is trying to figure out how the camera works, I'm just trying to figure out how I eat a slice of Black Forest gateau the size of my head.

Maria's sponge-tastic gift set the bar high and since then, no cake slice has rivalled that gateau. To this day, I've not eaten one as large or delicious. I'm not sure I ever will. Beyond the Black Forest, I continued to have no need for my camping mat, and the more miles I covered, the more grateful I became for the positive power of social media and the offers from European hosts. By the time the final public vote directed me to the shores of the Mediterranean at Marseille, I'd been on the road for 28 days and had been taken in to the homes of friendly strangers for 24 of those nights.

On the outskirts of Marseille, I took my sweet time gazing down on the sprawling suburbs from the hills just above them. It was a relief to be at the end of the journey, but also to be out of the snowy weather further north and to be riding in warmth and sunshine. I'd journeyed 1,327 miles since leaving London and travelled through four countries: the Netherlands, Germany, Switzerland and France.

Over the course of a month, more than 1,000 votes had been cast online and there was only one result that I hadn't been able to honour, when the public voted that I should pedal from Freiburg to the source of the Danube River at Donaueschingen. It began snowing heavily as I attempted to cycle over a mountain to reach the source. With the road covered in snow and my tyres sliding all over the place, I made the difficult decision to turn the bike around and head back to Freiburg. Once warm and dry, I let my followers know that I'd failed to make it to the Danube and posted some alternative voting options – ones that didn't involve me cycling over any mountains in the snow. I did feel a sense of responsibility to honour the time and effort that others had invested in supporting the journey. But if the adventure had taught me one thing, it was that it was never too late to change your mind. Even if you're halfway up a mountain and desperately want to make it to the other side. That mountain's not going anywhere.

In my month on the road, there was one thing that I regret not even considering. In fact, to this day, it's the only thing I regret from any adventure. On one voting post, an old work colleague went rogue and offered up a highly adventure-illegal fourth option. He wrote, 'Option 4. I fly you out to LA and you come and hang out with me and my husband in a hot tub and drink some wine in the Californian sunshine.' It might sound like a joke, but I know that man to be the kind of person who would have been very serious about the offer. But I turned it down. Why? Because I had planned to have an unplanned adventure in Europe, of course. You can't keep a good planner down.

So, did I get what I asked for – an adventure that made me mentally uncomfortable? Yes, ma'am. It was the most un-comfortable thing I've ever done. Did I learn that there's more than one way to skin an adventure cat? Absolutely. Would I do it again? Not on your nelly.

When I packed my bike into a box and loaded it onto a plane at Marseille Airport to fly home, I had no idea what life back in the UK would look like. I was heading to a new area of the country, as part of a new relationship, with no job to speak of and no friends nearby. But I had a feeling that taking a crash course in flying by the seat of your pants was a good way to ease me into the rocky road ahead. And, so long as I could find a way to focus on taking life just 24 hours at a time, then it would all be alright in the end. And who knows – perhaps, it would be better than alright.

Colleen
Yay, Miss Anna!! Thank you so much for the privilege of journeying alongside you. It has been fantastic!

Like · Reply ·

Susi
Anna - you gave me lots of great reminders of trips around Europe long forgotten - thanks for the rewind! Safe journey home!

Like · Reply ·

Victoria
Absolutely loved following your journey Anna and seeing where you ended up! 😊 As well as the interaction and part-participation that the voting / navigation allowed for. Enjoy the comforts of home when you get there. 😊

Like · Reply ·

Susan
Thanks Anna for letting us play. It's been fun.

Like · Reply ·

Danielle
Thank you for the vicarious adventure!

Like · Reply ·

Bridget
It's been so much fun. Can we do it again soon?

Like · Reply

A WELSH SURPRISE

Wales.
Winter, 2018.

It was a dreary Saturday afternoon in February and I had spent much of the weekend locked away in an office in my home city of Gloucester, putting the finishing touches to the draft of a new book. The strip lighting hurt my eyes, I had exhausted all available stashes of budget instant coffee and I was reaching the end of my writing tether. Thankfully, I was approaching the finish line of what had felt like a book-draft marathon. I slotted the final few words into place, gave the manuscript one final look-over and dropped it into an email to my favourite adventure editor.

Dearest Debbie,

Here it is! A first draft of 50 Shades of the USA. *It's not perfect. In fact, it's very far from perfect. Although I have cut 20,000 words of rubbish. So I do hope that it might be a bit less rubbish than it would have been, but that said, there will still be rubbish-ness lurking in there somewhere. Looking forward to your wonderful feedback and that honesty I love so much.*

Speak soon,

Anna xxx

I hit send, sat back from the computer and smiled. What a relief. Debbie would be working on the book for a few weeks, so there was nothing more that I could do now. Well, except treat myself to a mini adventure, and that was precisely what I had in mind.

I checked my watch. It was 3.30 p.m. Later than I'd hoped to finish. After hastily gathering my belongings from around the office, I ran down the stairs. There, waiting patiently for me in the hallway, softly lit by rays of afternoon sunlight streaming through the windows, was one of the most important women in my life. She looked gorgeous.

'Okay, Pauline. I'm done. Are you ready to go?' I asked. Pauline didn't reply. She was stoic like that, but I could tell by the bikepacking bags neatly nestled behind her saddle and handlebars that she was game for an adventure. We'd been adventuring together for over 10 years, after all – in the UK and in the mountains of Europe, too. When I needed her, Pauline was always there for me.

****

Having grown up in London and lived there until I was 30, I'd moved out west and into the countryside a few years ago. And yet I still couldn't get my head around the fact that I lived so close to Wales. The border was just 30 miles away, and

20 miles beyond that was the Brecon Beacons National Park. I'd nipped into the Beacons a few times by car, but hadn't yet explored them fully or taken advantage of the fact that they were within pedalling distance.

That Saturday, the plan was to cycle the 50 miles to the Beacons, grab a quick bite to eat somewhere en route and scramble up a hill to spend the night in my bivvy bag while watching the sunset. There, I would stay warm and toasty until Sunday morning when I would be greeted by a majestic sunrise. I would then go back down the mountain and pedal further into Wales for the day (say another 50 miles or so) and get the train home that evening. I would finish all of this in time to restart the madness of life on Monday morning. It was set to be just 24 little hours of escape. Twenty-four hours which I hoped would be a holiday for my brain from life's never-ending to-do list; instead, I'd treat it to some Brecon beauty, finding stillness in nature.

Overnight belongings crammed into bike bags, I wound my way through city streets and out of Gloucester, watching the whir of grey tarmac beneath my wheels and enjoying the warmth of the afternoon sun on my cheeks. Soon I crossed the River Severn and was surrounded by the tree giants in the Forest of Dean. I'd always found the forest to be a magical place – a dense pocket of green separating England from Wales, where moss clung to fallen branches and wild boar roamed free. The road through the forest was quiet, so I could hear the rustle of wind through the leaves and the trill of a lone song thrush, perched on the bough of a nearby oak tree.

There was a nip in the air now but, with every turn of the pedals, I felt freer – just a touch more in control and at ease with the constant go-go-go of life. I couldn't pack my worries with me on Pauline, after all – there was no room in her bags for those – so they'd been left behind in the city along with my to-do list. And that made me feel lighter, somehow. The space once consumed by all the things I felt I *should* be doing was now replaced by a sense of contentment with what I was *actually* doing at that very moment.

As I skirted the town of Monmouth and marvelled at the turrets of its historic castle, the sky began to glow in scarlet and purple as the last rays of orange stretched across the horizon and lazed beneath evening clouds. Once I was on the fringe of the Brecon Beacons National Park and in the shadow of the mountains themselves, the traffic thinned out. There were fewer and fewer passing cars until, finally, I was alone. Just Pauline and me on the road at dusk, caught somewhere between the real world I'd left behind and the adventure I imagined ahead of me.

By 6 p.m. it was dark and that was making me nervous. I'd hoped to be up one of the Beacons by now, having had a chance to get some ingredients for a mountain-top dinner and snuggled in my bivvy long before the sun set. Still, there wasn't much further to go – just 10 more miles to the foot of the climb and then I'd throw my bike on my shoulders and hike up to the top after that. I knew I'd have to do it all by torchlight, but I was sure that I'd pass a corner shop or a petrol station or something before then, so that I could grab some supplies for dinner.

I started up a small hill and saw a collection of lights at the top. At first I thought it must be houses, but as I got closer, I saw the unmistakable outline of a pub sign. 'No way!' I said aloud, squealing in delight at the prospect of scoring a hot dinner before heading up the hill to bed down for the night. It was dark now anyway – delaying the hike to the top by another hour wasn't going to change anything. And it would be worth it for some semi-decent food.

The pub was a modest-sized cream-coloured building with white sash windows and matching heavy white wooden doors. Fairy lights were strung between the trees out front and along a small wooden fence, which led to a garden around the back. The building looked in good condition so I hoped that it might be a modern kind of pub, as opposed to one that smelled of ale and wet dog with faded 70s carpet and gambling machines in the corner.

After wheeling my bike around the back, I locked it to some railings in the beer garden. I looked around and checked for passers-by before giving my armpits a quick sniff. They were still clinging on to a modicum of mustiness – the result of a day spent book editing followed by a hard ride into the countryside – but they didn't smell especially offensive. I glanced down at my Lycra-clad bottom half and noted that some of the mud from the road had splashed up onto my calves. *Ahh, that'll be fine*, I thought. So long as this wasn't a posh place, they wouldn't bat an eyelid.

Leaving my bike locked up in the garden, I followed the string of fairy lights around to the front of the pub and shoved open the white wooden door. The warmth of the place hit me immediately. And it wasn't just the temperature, it was everything – the smell of dinners bubbling away in the kitchen, the quiet chatter of a building full of people, the soft flicker of candles on tabletops. In stark contrast to the cold, still of the night, this pub was very much alive.

There were small seating areas on either side of where I was standing and, through a low doorway ahead, I could see a larger restaurant area, where all the 15 or so tables appeared to be full. In front of me was a short bar with a wooden top, and behind that bar was a man with dark hair. He was wearing a crisp white shirt and black trousers, and he was smiling. He was smiling at me.

'G'd evening, madam,' said the barman.

'Oh. Um… Good evening,' I replied.

'Have you made a reservation?' he asked.

'A reserv… oh. No. I was just hoping to grab some nosher, some dinner I mean… Is that okay?'

'But of course,' the barman nodded.

'Do you mind if I sit there?' I asked, gesturing to some seats at a wooden table to my right, by a flickering fire.

'You can indeed,' said the barman, before picking up a menu and leading me the three steps to the table.

'We're not serving dinner until seven,' he said as I sat down, 'but may I get you a drink before then? A glass of wine, perhaps?'

Ooohh lovely, I thought. I could definitely do with a glass of wine and, now that I was here, I fully intended to enjoy the experience. I was celebrating, after all!

'What have you got that's good? Wine-wise?' I asked.

'Ah! That would be a question for our sommelier. I'll have her come over.' Ooh, a sommelier – how fancy, I thought. A few minutes later, a young, dark-haired woman came over to the table. Her hair was fashioned into a neat ponytail, and she was wearing a white shirt and black trousers, just like the barman, but with the addition of studded diamanté earrings, which caught the light whenever she moved her head.

'Good evening, madam. I hear you would like to order a glass of wine?' said the woman.

'Yes, please. I most definitely would.'

'What kind do you like?'

'One that's red,' I said, and the woman smiled.

'Red. Yes. What kind of flavours do you enjoy?' she asked.

'Err.' I thought for a moment, racking my brain for something that sounded vaguely knowledgeable. 'Erm… Do you have any that taste like pudding in a cup?' The woman looked at me blankly. I forged on. 'You know, like a dessert. All sweet and sticky and syrupy and… delicious? One that I'd take a sip of and go "Oooo" and I'd feel it run all the way down my throat and into my belly. That kind of wine?' I said, and the woman smiled again.

'Ah. I see. Yes – we have a lovely bottle of Quinta do Vallado from Portugal. It's a two-thousand-and-nine. Red berries, slightly oaky, with a hint of nutmeg. Perfect for warming you up on a cold night like this one.'

'Ooh, I've never had wine from Portugal! I'll have a large glass of that then, please.'

With my hands wrapped around a glass of Portuguese vino-perfection, I sat by the fire for the next 45 minutes, waiting patiently for dinnertime. It wasn't quite the bivvy bag dining I'd expected, but I reasoned that I was still going to be adventurous and sleep up a mountain after this, so I would allow the unexpected pub stopover.

At five minutes to seven, the barman came back to the table.

'A small gift from the chef,' he said, placing a side plate in front of me and setting a tiny fork next to it. On the plate was what looked like an arancini rice ball, with breadcrumbs on the outside, and it was sitting on a splodge of tomatoey sauce.

'Oh, I don't think I ordered this,' I said, feeling embarrassed that there'd been some confusion.

'No madam – it's a gift. An appetiser. Here we have wild rice delicately cooked in spring water from the local mountains, mixed with chopped wild woodland mushrooms, sage and crushed garlic, fused into a sphere. It's been lightly cooked, once in white wine and then again in walnut oil. On the top of the sphere are flakes of Parmesan cheese and truffle shavings from the nearby forest, which add to the smoky flavour…'

The barman went on to tell me everything about the life of the rice ball. After a minute, I zoned out, wondering how it was possible to cram so many ingredients into something so tiny. When the barman was gone, I picked the ball-thing up. I inspected it for a moment before popping it into my mouth, whole. I supposed that I was meant to nibble at it or something. Or perhaps bite the top off and lick out the centre – that's how I ate my Cadbury's Creme Eggs, after all. But I was hungry and this was food and I now had a belly full of Portuguese wine that needed soaking up before I climbed a mountain.

A few minutes later, the barman returned. 'Are you ready to order your dinner?' he asked. Oh crikey! In all my relaxing I'd completely forgotten to look at the menu. I picked up the single page of cream card he'd handed me and gave it a brief skim. Blimey. The menu was posh. I knew it was posh because they didn't capitalise the first letters of any of the dishes and there were no full stops anywhere. I made some hasty decisions and swiftly ordered some pasta, which was the cheapest thing on the menu. I then ordered a side of broccoli, because I didn't want the barman to think that I was being tight and ordering the cheapest thing on the menu (which, of course, I was).

At 9 p.m., with a belly full of rice ball, pasta and broccoli,

I paid the surprisingly modest bill, thanked the barman for his hospitality and the sommelier for her recommendation for Portuguese 'pudding in a cup', and left the pub. It had now started to rain and I wondered quite why I had thought that it was a good idea to sleep on top of a Brecon Beacon in the middle of February. I could be at home right now, curled up on my sofa, binging on Netflix, but instead I was heading out into the rain.

Grumbling at the turn in weather, I hopped back on Pauline and pedalled off down the road, straining to reach the handlebars over a belly full of pub fare and convinced that the 100 ingredients in the rice ball had expanded the moment they hit my stomach. A few miles past the pub, I took a turn off at a gravel car park and followed a rubble lane to the foot of the mountain. I got off my bike and, not wanting to leave Pauline alone at the bottom, hauled her up onto my shoulders for a 45-minute clamber to the top.

During that slog, I repeatedly reminded myself that it would all be worth it come the morning. It was always such a treat to bed down somewhere new in the darkness and then wake at sunrise to see everything that had been covered by a blanket of stars the night before.

Of course, dreams are fragile things. They evaporate into thin air, or rather reality, the moment you reach them. I didn't get the serene hilltop slumber I'd hoped for. Instead, it tipped with rain the whole night and I shivered as a strong, icy wind whipped across the mountain top, cutting straight through the bivvy bag and chilling me to the bone. When I opened my eyes at dawn, a wall of grey cloud had kidnapped my spectacular mountain-top sunrise – it was nowhere to be seen.

Accepting that I wasn't going to get that great view I was after, I began slipping and sliding my way back down the mountain, struggling to stay upright while carrying Pauline on my back. I soon decided that a better strategy was to slide all the way to the bottom on my bum, so that's just what I did.

Once I made it back to the gravel car park, it started to rain again. I briefly thought back to the original Sunday plan, which had been to cycle for a further 50 miles, deeper into Wales. I was cold, I was wet, and my lower half was now caked in mud. The rain had soaked through my down jacket (which would take a month of Sundays to dry) and I was starting to shiver. 'Screw this!' I said aloud. I was always one for surprise and adventure, but I felt like this was an ambush. I'd had enough 'adventure' in the past 12 hours to last me a good while yet. So, instead of cycling for a day in the rain, I followed signs into the nearest town of Abergavenny, pedalled straight to the train station and bundled Pauline onto the train back to Gloucester.

****

That afternoon, having enjoyed a hot shower and wolfed down a hot lunch – which was comprised of just three ingredients, not ten – I clambered into my sheep onesie (because it was the only thing I had clean that would get me warm quickly) and curled up on the rug by the wood burner in my flat.

I'd been meaning to find out more about the mysterious pub I'd stumbled upon the previous night and was now wondering whether I had imagined it all. Was it like a mirage in the desert? Had I gone crazy while writing my book and conjured up the pub and its delicious nosh in my mind? Lying on my side in the sheep onesie, enjoying the warmth of a flickering fire, I googled the pub's name. As it turned out, that Saturday night in February, I'd eaten dinner, in my Lycra, with my mud-spattered calves and musty armpits, at the Michelin-starred Walnut Tree Inn. Well, I never. Mud and Michelin – I couldn't think of a better unexpected combination for an overnight Welsh adventure.

LITTLE ADVENTURES
AROUND THE BIG SMOKE

London.
Summer, 2014.

In my late 20s I was living in London – working a 9-to-5 and doing my best to stay sane in a world of concrete, corporations, noise, pollution and people, while restocking a hideously depleted bank balance. Having spent much of the previous year pedalling a bike around the USA, time at home spent saving up for the next great escape was necessary, but it was frustrating, nonetheless. And so, in a bid to stave off the adventure-itchies, which I'd recently contracted, I'd taken to reading countless travel books and going to public talks about adventures in the evenings after work. Both things had led me to the conclusion that adventures don't always have to be grand journeys to far-flung places. Adventure is more about mindset than where in the world you are, after all. You can have the most magical adventure in the space of an afternoon, an evening, or even overnight in the middle of the week – experiences that the British adventurer Alastair Humphreys has labelled 'microadventures'.

The concept of a microadventure is simple: leave work at 5 p.m. sharp, grab a chum (or two or three) and escape to the countryside. Then eat, laugh, indulge in a wee dram, sleep under the stars and be back at your desk the following morning for that 9 a.m. team meeting. Perhaps with a faint whiff of *eau du field* about your person and a dirty little secret to boot, but smiling from ear to ear.

And so, while walking home from work one night, I had (even if I do say so myself) a rather good idea. Over the following couple of months, I would explore just how easy it might be to squeeze in adventure around a full-time, corporate job in London. I'd drag as many other city slickers as I could along for the adventuresome, wild-sleeping ride and do one overnight trip per week, in each of the six counties that surround the city – Berkshire, Buckinghamshire, Hertfordshire, Essex, Kent and Surrey (and yes, I did have to google them). Then, for the *pièce de résistance*, during the final week, I'd find a way for us all to sleep out in Greater London itself.

Was I mad? Quite possibly. Would anyone actually join in? Who knew. Would I be sleeping wild for those seven nights on my own? I was prepared for that to be the case. Nevertheless, I announced the idea on social media, sent emails and texts to outdoors-loving friends and waited for their replies.

****

The first microadventure mission took place on a Wednesday night in June near Henley-on-Thames. Henley is technically in Oxfordshire, but if you cross the bridge on the outskirts of town you are magically transported into the neighbouring county of... Berkshire. And the group of adventurers assembled on the Berkshire riverbank would have made the Avengers proud – largely thanks to the special individuals who'd answered the call to the wild. First of all, there was Will, a friend who once set off on a seven-year cycle tour around the world, dressed as his alter ego, Super Cycling Man. Will pedalled to Berkshire from London in his superhero suit but was stopped, for photos, so many times by passers-by that he was late and almost missed dinner. Shropshire natives and married couple Laraine and Owain (yes, I think it's cute that their names rhyme, too) rolled into Henley by car – looking glamorous in the clothes that they'd worn at a charity awards event that afternoon. A cameraman called Mark jetted in from Jersey, Jo (a friend who had once rollerbladed around Amsterdam with me) arrived from the north of England, and the rest of us, well, the rest of us… got the train from the centre of London. How dull.

By the time a nine-strong team were gathered in the beer garden at The Little Angel pub with bevvies in hand, we represented a neat cross section of society. Workers from health and safety, finance, performing arts, education, courier services and communications were all there, ready to shirk responsibility, cast off the 9 to 5 and (as Al Humphreys puts it) start living for the 5 to 9 instead.

After consuming a mix of carbs and protein (burger = protein, bun = carbs), and one of our five-a-day (there was a gherkin in the burger), hydrating ourselves (by quaffing local ales) and making sure we had adequately warmed up our muscles (by playing Jenga), we left the pub at 9 p.m. and set out on the Chiltern Way footpath in darkness. Guided by my trusty headtorch, which contained the fire of a thousand suns, I accidentally blinded my wild camping buddies at intervals as we picked our way across fields, through gates and over stiles (much to Super Cycling Man's despair, as he had to hoick his bike over each one). Twenty minutes later we arrived at a clearing in a nearby wood with just enough space for nine weary bodies to rest.

'I need to hang my bag in the tree,' announced my ever-cautious rollerblading friend Jo, as we began laying out our bivvy bags.

'Errr, okay – why?' I asked.

'It's got my banana bread in it.'

'Ah okay, that makes sen… no, wait. Why does it need to go in the tree?'

'Because… I don't know… there might be bears, or something,' she replied.

After reassuring Lady Jo that the only likely candidate for a banana bread predator in Henley was a rogue badger, we unrolled mats, shimmied into pyjamas and went for one last gawd-I-hope-it-lasts-till-morning pee. We burrowed deep into our sleeping bags and snuggled up under a canopy of trees and fragmented moonlight. The soft chatter between friends turned to whispers as each of us drifted off to sleep, one by one, on our first mini adventure, together and within sniffing distance of London.

The following morning, I woke up at 5.30 a.m. and slid as silently as I could out of my bivvy bag. Tiptoeing over sleeping bodies, I headed out of the woods to check out our surroundings. Dawn was just beginning to break and bronze-coloured light had diffused across the sky beyond the wood. I stepped out of the trees and let my eyes adjust. Wowsers. I was standing on the edge of a poppy field – a sea of red petals fluttering on long stalks in the morning breeze. I stood for 10 minutes and drank in the scene, feeling greedy to have something so beautiful all to myself.

By the time I returned to camp, my fellow wilderness explorers were awake. Jetboil stoves were fired up, a timely brew was… brewed, and a breakfast of banana bread and croissants was consumed – all of which had miraculously survived any attack from the Henley bears. With bellies full, we shoved our gear back into our packs and ambled out of the woods, taking a different return route to the train station, along the River Thames. Morning light danced across the surface of the water and made the river look inviting, so we then did what any civilised Berkshire resident would do at 6 a.m.: cannonballed into the Thames in our pants (in the case of Super Cycling Man his pants were, naturally, on the outside of his clothing). Plunging into the cool water was a shock to the system but, hands down, the best way to bring every cell of your body to life in an instant. We squealed, frolicked, swam and sang, before getting out of the river and scurrying, still wet, to the train station. Then we caught the 7 a.m. train back to London, and back to normal life.

The Berkshire bivvy bag extravaganza was just the beginning. As the weeks rumbled by, I was amazed as more and more people signed up to join in my mini-adventure experiment. There seemed to be some kind of mystical power to a set of instructions that read 'Meet me under the clock at the train station at 6.30 p.m. Bring your debit card, sleeping gear and some snacks. We'll be back by 8 a.m. the following morning.' Each Wednesday night I'd have a group of between 5 and 15 people join me. Sign-ups became so popular that I had to start turning people away – big groups would alter the zen of the wilderness vibe we were so desperately seeking, after all. Still, it was undeniable – the concept of city-centric adventures was a rolling stone, and it was gathering pace.

It wasn't long before I started to feel pressure to find memorable places to take my fellow Londoners each week – many of whom had never wild-camped before. I took to searching online for things like 'best views in (insert county)', 'highest points in…', 'lakes and rivers in…' And, in a bid to guarantee a breathtaking sunset vista, I even branched out to researching the 'most romantic spots'. Ooh-err. I also discovered a lesser-known resource called Slopehunter – one of the best-kept secrets for finding hilltops to sleep on in the south-east of England. This site describes and rates the hills, lets you know how to get there, who owns the land and what the 'lift' is like, should you wish to launch a small plane (who doesn't these days?).

An overnight trip to Hadleigh Castle during the third week turned out to be a real gem of a wild night out. It took just 38 minutes for seven of us to travel by train from the centre of London to Leigh-on-Sea in Essex for the night. It wasn't long before I was tucked up in my bivvy bag, on a gentle slope below the ruins of the reddish-brown Hadleigh Castle, with a clear 180-degree view of the surrounding land. As the sun slid below the horizon, its long rays were replaced with a faint twinkle of street lights in the distance and, as the early evening glow unfolded around me, I realised I was glowing inside too. We were just a stone's throw from the city and I could feel its incessant go-go-go tugging at the recesses of my mind, but I had escaped the rat race. I had beaten the system. I had won at life, if only for a few precious hours.

I shut my eyes and listened. Never before had I been so acutely aware of how the sounds around me were changing. I fell asleep to the noise of a man-made orchestra: the rumble of planes overhead, a dull hum of traffic from the A13 not far behind us, a train horn and the clackety-clack of wheels on the track below. Night-time gave way to virtual silence, with only the rustle of leaves and whistles through the long grass to disturb our dreams. When the light of the moon faded and a pink sunrise took hold, I was woken by a lone bird. Then another, and another, until a full-blown cacophony made it impossible to sleep any longer. Eventually, the first city-bound train thundered past, the hum of the A road returned and planes cut across the sky overhead. It was now 6 a.m. We'd come full circle and it was time to get back to work.

After Essex and Berkshire, I continued to tick off the counties one by one. In Buckinghamshire, 10 of us sat side by side on the fallen trunk of an old oak tree, on a steep hill over-looking a suburb, tending to a small fire, sipping hot choc-olate, sharing Percy Pig sweets and picnic nibbles until long after dark. In Kent, an especially excitable group got a history fix by taking a tour of a Roman fort before falling asleep in a field nearby. In the morning we watched dew drops slowly drip from tips of long grass, before stripping to our under-wear and body-surfing down a local stream on our inflatable camping mats. In Hertfordshire, we enjoyed a group picnic on a hillside while watching purple and peach-coloured clouds gather around a slowly setting summer sun. We retreated to some nearby woods to sleep and ate doughnuts for breakfast. Oxfordshire served up a night to remember because it tipped with rain for much of the evening. But that didn't stop one talented adventurer from serenading us with his guitar – his dulcet tones soothing tired bodies until the grey clouds above us cleared and the sky was filled with stars.

When it came to doing a sleep-out in Surrey, I was con-cerned it would be difficult to find a special camp spot. I'd grown up in Surrey and so could have brushed it off as too familiar to be worth the visit. But I had learned that this is what small adventures are all about – seeing the world through fresh eyes. Visiting places you believe you know like the back of your hand and being surprised at what you find there. Path-ways, once invisible, leading to woods that have been, until now, unseen.

Keeping things in 'the faaaaamily' (to be said in a mob mafia accent), the Surrey excursion included a cameo from wild-camping rookie, chartered accountant, sensible soul and all-round suburban gent, my brother – Jonty McNuff. Jonty met me and Super Cycling Man Will (you remember him) at a corner of Richmond Park. Super Cycling Man had brought spare capes for Jonty and me (as you do), so we three caped crusaders set off on bikes through south-western suburbia and out into quiet country lanes amid soft birdsong… the whir of wheels… and beats of the 90s blasting from Will's water-bottle boom box. Following an appetiser of samosas and strawberry milkshakes at a local Michelin-starred restaurant called 'Le Shell Petrol Garage', we headed to The Queen's Head pub for the main course. Once thirsts were quenched and hungers satisfied, we pootled up a nearby steep hill and took a footpath across a field into a nearby public wood.

It was only after setting up camp that I realised I'd left my phone in the pub. I let out a long sigh and headed off alone for a 2-mile round trip to collect it. As I made my way back through the woods, I spotted a neighbouring farm close by. I hadn't noticed it earlier but, now that darkness had fallen, I could see its lights shining through the trees. When I arrived at camp, I told the boys that our sleeping spot wasn't so wild after all and we made a concerted effort to keep our voices down and any twig-cracking to a minimum. It didn't do to draw any unwanted attention, after all. Just then…

BRRRRRRRRRIIIIIIIILNNNNNNNNNNNGGGGGGGG!!

My phone slashed through the silence. I scrambled to locate it, hoping I could find it before the second ring, and answered just in time:

'Hello...?' I said.

'Hello!' came a familiar voice, accompanied by a tone that told me I was in trouble.

'Oh. Hi Mum.'

'Hi indeed. Where are you, petal?'

'In the woods, Mum. Like I told you.'

'Is your brother there?'

'Yes.'

'And you're alright?'

'Yes.'

'Thank goodness. I thought that something had happened...' she continued.

Unfortunately, in the time it had taken me to cycle back down to retrieve my phone and return to camp, the pub had called the 'home' landline number they'd found in my phone. Mum had dialled 1571 (to see who had called her) – who even does that anymore? – and when they picked up they informed her that her daughter had forgotten her phone and left the pub sometime earlier with two men. She'd called Jonty but got no answer from his phone so Mum, as only mothers do, had convinced herself that both Jonty and I had been kidnapped by a strange man in the depths of leafy Surrey.

Mum's worries laid to rest, it was time for bed. I lay

awake for longer than usual, staring up at the ceiling of leaves and discovered that I could unfocus my eyes just enough to make-believe that the gaps of light in the canopy were hundreds of stars. As night unfolded, Jonty was eaten alive by an array of flying insects, a slug (called Samuel) took up residence on Super Cycling Man's hand, and I listened to several nearby foxes having sex or a fight – I couldn't decide which. Morning brought the most spectacular scarlet dawn. We de-camped from the woods to an open field and watched the world wake up from our thrones of smugness. Hot chocolates in hand, croissants mid-dunk, we enjoyed a cracking view all the way into the city – where we would soon be heading back to work.

****

Come the seventh week of the mini-adventure mission, I had become accustomed to (as one mate put it) 'spending my evenings sleeping in bushes with friends and strangers', but at last, it was time to take on the mini mothership – a sleep-out in Greater London itself. On the final Wednesday of the project, 40 fully employed, self-respecting city slickers with perfectly decent homes to go to assembled in the cellar bar of a West End pub. By 9 p.m., our bellies were bulging with pub fare and we split into small groups to prepare for journeys to various small pockets of wilderness around London.

The scene that unfolded in the alley outside The Pontefract Castle pub in Soho would have made any big corporate's HR team-building department dribble with delight. Groups of relative strangers huddled together over smartphones – browsers open on London transport apps, Google Maps and supermarket store locators – discussing how to make their way to their assigned locations, where they would sleep, and (crucially) where they might stop to buy an evening drink and brekkie for the morning. We wished one another luck and departed with our groups – bound for our chosen adventure spots.

I was heading up a North London elite squadron of three, which consisted of me and two friends, both named Andy. It was long past dark by the time I settled down in the middle of an Andy *mandwich* on a hill in front of the iconic Victorian Alexandra Palace. All three of us sat on a single camping mat and put the world to rights with cups of peppermint tea in hands – gazing at the spikes and curves of the London skyline. We identified the city landmarks as best we could but there was a long debate about what the 'semi-jagged, mid-height slopey thing' was to the east. Every now and then social media would offer up a glimpse of what other groups were up to on their own nights out in the capital. Team Hampstead Heath seemed to have gone a little OTT on the refreshments (it was like a mobile wine store up there); there was a wonderful nighttime vista shared from Primrose Hill; and it seemed that Team Richmond Park had experienced quite an adventure already, just trying to find and enter the park.

I'd be lying if I didn't confess to some subtle differences between a camp-out in Greater London and the previous, more rural, locations. In North London, at least, the soft rustle of the wind through the tree leaves was frequently disturbed by a 20-something chundering in the bushes. The brilliance of the stars was partially dampened by light pollution and a police siren would ring out through the still night air every now and then. But there was a deep sense of triumph and satisfaction to be had from finding even a modicum of serenity in an area populated by nine million people. This was London – warts 'n' all – and with every sunrise and sunset I took the time to witness, I grew ever fonder of its quirks.

****

I enjoyed the seven weeks of mini-adventures so much that I carried on sleeping wild in forests, on shorelines, around lakes and by rivers each Wednesday night for 25 consecutive weeks. After six months of exploring counties around London, I hung up my bivvy bag, happy in the knowledge that not only had I got to know London's outer limits a little better, but I'd also helped over 200 others do the same.

At a time when, all too often, our daily lives are unwittingly filled with activities that don't stay long in the mind, small overnight adventures make memories. There's no cheaper and

more accessible way to reinstil a sense of wonder for local places that you've foolishly convinced yourself are wonder-less.

No grandad will ever sit a toddler on his knee, offer up a
hard-boiled Werther's Original and tell of the time he went
home from work, collapsed exhausted into a chair and flicked
on season four, episode three of *Game of Thrones*. Daenerys
Stormborn will set her dragons on me for that, but it's true.
But that time you went to camp on a hilltop, chatted idly with
a group of new friends as you drifted off to sleep in the long
grass beneath the stars…? Now that – that might just make
the cut.

THE SNOW-TIPPED
SILENCE

Canada.
Winter, 2017.

It's 8 a.m. on the Trans-Canada Highway and we're heading west. It's still dark outside and cold too, around –30°C, and the blackish green evergreens that line our route are dusted with snow – spiky tops whizzing past the window at full size but getting smaller and smaller until they disappear behind us. I've got a coffee in my hand, there's country music playing on the radio, and the road ahead of us is straight. In fact, I can't remember the last time we rounded a bend.

I look into the passenger wing mirror and catch sight of the sun beginning to rise behind us in the east. Swirls of scarlet and tangerine are fused with a backdrop of midnight blue, making the image in the wing mirror a precious snapshot in time – a quiet moment on the threshold between night and day. Delicate frost crystals have formed around the edges of the mirror so that the sunrise within it appears like a painting with a glistening white frame. It's a work of art that I'd like hang above my mantlepiece and look at in years to come, when I want to be transported to another time and place.

NEWFIE LOVE

Once upon a time, in a land not so far away called planet Earth, my partner in crime, Jamie, decided to run 5,000 miles across Canada dressed as a superhero. Soon after finishing that journey, he released a book about his trans-Canada jogette (called *Adventureman: Anyone Can Be a Superhero*). The release of that book seemed like the perfect excuse for another 5,000-mile trip across the country – although this time we'd travel together in a minivan, disguising the journey as 'work' by doing a book tour while we travelled.

The plan was to retrace Jamie's steps as closely as we could, starting on the wild and rocky Atlantic shores of Newfoundland in the east and finishing up beside the Pacific Ocean on Vancouver Island in the west. We hoped that the journey across the land of moose and maple leaves would take five months or so and, to add some adventure-spice to the mix, we'd decided to do it in winter. Phwooooar.

It was early November when we touched down across the waters of the Atlantic Ocean and our first port of call was the home of Mark and Mary Ploughman, who live in St John's, Newfoundland – North America's most easterly city. It was the first time I'd visited their home but Jamie had been there before. Way back in 2013, he'd sat next to a stranger called Mary on a flight from Toronto to St John's.

'What brings you to Newfoundland?' Mary had asked.

'I'm running across Canada,' Jamie replied.

'Well, do you have anywhere to stay tonight?' she asked. Jamie shook his head, and the rest is history. Just as Mary and Mark had taken a naive young lad from Gloucester under their wing all those years ago, this time they'd spread their hosting wings extra wide so that I could snuggle up under them too.

Newfoundland wasn't a place I knew much about until we began planning for the trip but, the more I read about it, the more it intrigued me. Separated from the Canadian mainland by the Strait of Belle Isle, the island goes by the nickname 'The Rock' – a name that has nothing to do with the world-famous wrestler turned Hollywood superstar, but aptly describes the wild and windswept scenery on the island. Grey boulders and wind-battered trees dominate the landscape and, with a relatively small population living on a 'rock' that's 250 miles across, there's a whole lot of wide-open space.

On our first morning in St John's, I peeled open my eyes and forgot for a moment where I was. I'd been stirred from my slumber by the whistle of the wind sneaking through the gaps in the wooden window frames but was I warm and snug under three layers of fleecy blankets in a soft double bed. Beyond the window, peeping from under the blankets, I could see one large tree and several smaller ones – a few clusters of red and orange late-autumn leaves clinging to otherwise barren branches and being battered by the unforgiving North Atlantic wind.

I nudged Jamie awake and it wasn't long before we were enticed out of bed by the smell of coffee and freshly cooked bacon. Keen to investigate the source of the breakfast aroma, Jamie and I tiptoed down the wooden stairs and into the kitchen. Mark was standing by the stove in a white apron, armed and dangerous – spatula in hand. 'Morning kids! How does pancakes for breakfast sound?' he beamed. Mark is an engineer by trade, but a chef at all other times.

Over the course of the following week at the Ploughman's in St John's, we travelled around the world from the comfort of their dinner table, visiting a new country each night. Monday came with a treat of fish tacos (with cod caught on nearby Fogo Island), which was followed by a wild chanterelle mushroom risotto (the mushrooms having been foraged up in Labrador). Local Atlantic mussels in a Thai red curry sauce were the starter for a Tuesday feast of fresh sushi, and then there was a BBQ smoked steak on Wednesday night. Mark said that food always tasted better when there was a story attached to it, so each meal came with a tale of adventure, and, just when we thought our evening meals couldn't get any better, Mary steamed in on Thursday with her own story and a New York-style cheesecake. Well played, Mary, well played.

On Friday evening at Casa Ploughman, over yet another a tasty dinner (deep-fried risotto balls with lashings of Parmigiano), Jamie and I decided to check in on the status of our pre-road-trip to-do list. There was still a lot to get sorted before we started the westward journey across the country, but the number-one item at the top of the list was collecting our adventure wagon. The owners of our recently purchased minivan lived in Embree, a small town on the north coast of

Newfoundland. I looked up Embree on the map. It was a five-hour drive from St John's.

'Oh, I'll take you there. It's just down the road,' said Mark, casually. Jamie and I looked up from the map and at one another. I pulled a face that said 'We can't let him do that'.

'Oh no, don't worry, Mark. We'll get a hire car or something. It's… five hours away… that's a ten-hour round trip,' I said.

'Nonsense. Like I said… that's just down the road,' Mark smiled.

Canadians – you've gotta love 'em.

It was love at first sight with our adventure wagon. We called her Magster, which was short for Maggie – the name of an exceptionally kind Canadian woman who had played a huge role in drumming up support for Jamie during his trans-Canada run. Believe it or not, Maggie had insisted on buying the minivan for us, with instructions to sell it and donate the money to Jamie's charity when we reached Vancouver. Magster was navy blue, with six seats, red and yellow detail on the dashboard, and red hubs on the wheels. She was rusty in some places but perfect in every other way. We drove back to St John's to spend one final night with Mark and Mary. I squeezed them extra tight before we left the following morning and, from the moment we turned the keys in Magster's ignition, I was overwhelmed with a sense of freedom. There were 5,000 miles of highway in front us and nothing but the Atlantic Ocean behind us.

Over the next few weeks, we moved swiftly from one town to the next, stopping briefly for Jamie to give talks in local venues and to stay with the warm-hearted people who had supported him on his run. We were treated to wine, beer and three-course meals in each house, which made it feel more like visiting relatives than road-trippin' between the homes of strangers. In a bid to combat our ever-expanding waistlines, Jamie and I took it in turns to throw one another out of the car to run on forest trails alongside the Trans-Canada High-way, meeting up with the other person at the next gas station. During these runs, I kept an eye out for moose. I knew there were thousands of them on the island and, when Jamie turfed me out of the Magster for a run, I always half-hoped that I would see one and half-hoped that I wouldn't. I'd met a moose once before, in Alaska, and I knew that they were ginormous and intimidating, but majestic too. I settled on the idea that I'd quite like to see one at a distance, but that never happened. The best I came back with was sightings of moose prints in the snow.

As we drove across Newfoundland, we passed through the towns of Holyrood, Blaketown, Clarenville, Port Blandford and (my fave) a place called Come By Chance. Ooh-err. We also took a side trip to the town of Dildo. Because. Well, just because. I can confirm that Dildo is a lovely place.

Spurred on by novel place names and flasks of weak take-away coffee, we made good headway west and were three quarters of the way across Newfoundland when I decided that we'd earned a day off from driving. It was time to do some exploring instead.

'There's a park to the north called Gros Morne… It's got a mountain in the middle of it,' said I to Jamie.

'Sounds lovely, my dear. Let's go,' said he to me. And off we went.

Early the following morning we trundled down a gravel track to a car park at the foot of Gros Morne mountain. There were no other cars around and I started to wonder whether we were idiots to head up a mountain in the middle of winter, but I shoved those thoughts aside. I tucked some honey sandwiches into our packs, took one last glug of coffee and we set off down the trail – under cloudy skies and in light rain, for a 9-mile round trip to the summit and back.

It was a cold morning and the temperature began to drop as we weaved our way through light forest to a fork in the trail. The air was whipping at our already frozen, reddened cheeks and the tip of my nose had started to tingle in the chill. We took the left-hand track, around the base of Gros Morne, before starting the ascent up the north side of the mountain. Soon, the rocks beneath our feet became a mix of scree-like stones and large red-grey boulders dominated the trail ahead.

We pushed onwards and upwards, past small shrubs and chest-high trees – many were just bare branches, but others had clumps of wind-ravaged green on show, the pine needles doing what they could to survive the harsh conditions. Four miles into the hike, we started up a small gulley which was filled with a thick fog. I stopped to watch how it moved – a pallid soup of white and grey rolling over the ridge to the west, behaving just as steam would on the top of a witch's cauldron.

Further up the gulley, the climb steepened and the wind picked up. Gradually the trees disappeared entirely, until the only vegetation among a sea of rock were straw-coloured tufts of grass and brown-red shrubs – all of their branches encased in ice. I couldn't believe how intricate the shrub sculptures were. Each one appeared to be fighting the good fight on the exposed face of Gros Morne, tinkling and cracking as we passed, shattering like glass.

Despite the wind, there was a stillness in the air which made the ice-encrusted gulley feel eerie. And, if I'm honest, it freaked me out. We hadn't seen anyone in two hours of hiking and it was getting colder by the minute. There was more snow and ice too, making the trail slippery underfoot. The still air and worsening conditions caused my imagination to run wild. *What if we shouldn't be up here in winter? What if the trail up ahead is too slippery? What if we make the top but then can't get back down safely?*

The trail kicked up steeply again so that we were now scrambling on our hands and knees through the snow. I was busy doing battle with my imagination and just beginning to wonder if things were tipping over to the wrong side of dicey when my head popped over the top of a rocky lip and my jaw dropped.

'Oh. My. Word,' I said aloud, standing up and staring. 'Jamie! Jamie! Get up here – you have to see this!' I called back down the trail. I had made it to the summit of Gros Morne.

The terrain in front of me had flattened out and I was now on an icicle-encrusted plateau. For as far as I could see, the land was white, a mixture of frost and snow, as if someone had exploded a bag of glitter and it had coated every square inch of the land. I was still surrounded by fog, but it was clearing, and the sun was beginning to peek through, which made the pearly white ground glisten.

'Woah!' said Jamie, appearing behind me and pausing briefly to catch his breath. 'That is insane!'

'Isn't it?' I said, letting out a long sigh. I crunched over the snow on the plateau without saying anything else, propelled, or so it felt, by a will that wasn't my own. It was the will of the mountain – pure and powerful.

For the next 10 minutes, we ran around at the top of the mountain like giddy school kids, taking photos and inspecting frozen plants – doing our best to record the experience but, all the while, knowing that we couldn't possibly capture *this*. Not through a camera lens anyway. It was a landscape that only the richness of a memory could do justice to.

We were midway through congratulating ourselves for such a bold and daring decision to climb a mountain in winter when a new sight on the horizon stopped me in my tracks.

'What in the world?'

'Rainbow!' shouted Jamie.

'Raaaiiiinboooowwwww!' I hollered back. Except… it didn't look like any rainbow I'd ever seen before. And then I realised. 'FOGGGGBOWWWW!' I yelled, even louder this time.

'Whhhat?' said Jamie, confused.

'A fogbow – look… it's come out of the fog,' I said, pointing to the wall of grey that we'd been climbing through to make the summit.

I'd never seen a fogbow before. I'd only ever heard about them and I had always wondered if they were mythical things, like unicorns. A fogbow is similar to a rainbow, but it forms, not when light passes through rain but, instead, when light passes through fog. The smaller water droplets of the fog mean that the colours of the bow are muted, so much so that fogbows are often called 'white rainbows'. Although, in the fogbow in front of us, I could clearly see ghostly arcs of red and blue on either curve of the arch. The whiteness in between added a luminescent glow that made the fogbow all the more majestic.

We stood and marvelled at the bodacious bow for a few more minutes, unwilling to drag ourselves away, watching rays of sun dance along the stream of pale colours in that beautiful full arc across a grey-blue sky. I have a photo that Jamie took of me in that moment; I'm standing beneath the fogbow in a pair of blue leggings and a black coat, arms outstretched, my glove-covered hands reaching up towards the arc, fingertips almost touching its other-worldly magic.

****

Three weeks into our trans-Canada journey, but still in Newfoundland, we found ourselves staying with locals Anne and Tony in the town of Corner Brook. I loved Anne's energy, her endearing Irish-American Newfoundland accent and her ability to speak at a million miles an hour (as many Newfies do). Tony brought a laid-back vibe to the party and, on account of his name and dark Mediterranean features, we began referring to him as 'The Godfather'.

It was during our stay at Anne and Tony's that our immersion in Newfoundland culture tipped up a notch. They were hell-bent on helping us become fluent in Newfinese. Having mastered some basic terms like 'yes b'y', which means 'I agree', and 'best kind', meaning 'I like that, it's good,' we were ready to take things to the next level. It was time to get 'screeched in'. Screeched what? Screeched in, I tell you. All the kids were doing it. Well, all the British kids who wanted to be made honorary Newfoundlanders were doing it, and that was us.

We visited the home of one of Anne's relatives for the special 'screeching in' ceremony, and one of the youngsters of the family set the musical tone by playing an Irish jig on her violin. Post jiggin' around the dining room, Anne's sister-in-law asked Jamie and me: 'De yer want to be a Newfoundlander?' To which we replied a hearty, 'Yes b'y!'

With each of us holding a shot of Screech (which is a kind of rum), Jamie and I were asked, 'Are ye a screecher?' We gave the proper response, which is: 'Deed I is, me ol' cock! And long may yer big jib draw!' Which means 'Yes, I am, my old friend, and may your sails always catch wind.' We then drank our shots of Screech, ate a salted fish head and some cold meat (which I tried not to chuck straight back up), danced around a bit, put on a yellow fisherman's hat, kissed a dead fish on the lips (no tongues, of course), drank another shot of Screech and the ceremony was complete. We were presented with a certificate and were now officially NEWFIES! And my mouth would taste of salty fish forevermore.

A few days after the screeching ceremony, we had just about got over the excitement of kissing a salted cod and were staying in the town of Channel-Port aux Basques and preparing to leave Newfoundland. I was midway through spooning cereal into my mouth when there was a knock at our motel room door. It was Anne, our Corner Brook host, teacher of Newfinese and proud screecher-innner. She was holding a moose. Yes, you heard me – she was holding… a moose. Okay, it was a soft toy, but it was massive and moosey all the same.

'G' mornin'!' she said in that beautiful Newfie accent.

'Anne! What are you doing here?' I asked.

'Well… I was watching all yer posts about the moose tracks on yer runs and having not seen one 'n' all, even when you went up the Morne, and it gots me to thinkin'…'

'You're dangerous when you get thinking, Anne,'

Jamie interrupted.

'I know. Now pipe down will ya, boy!' Anne said, and Jamie grinned. 'Tony and I decided that we can't be having you leave Newfoundland without having seen a moose… Not now that you're real Newfies. So, I boughts ya one.'

She held out the stuffed moose towards us and we engulfed her and the moose in one giant bear hug… or rather moose hug.

'Aw, thanks, Anne! Best present ever,' I said.

'Just promise me you'll look after him all the way to Vancouver now?'

'Promise,' I replied.

And so, Jamie, Monty the Moose and I piled into Magster the minivan, each with a coffee in our hands (a latte for Monty) and waved goodbye to a place and people that had grown dear to our hearts. We boarded a ferry across the Gulf of St Lawrence, bound for Nova Scotia on our journey west across the mighty land of Canada.

BLIZZARD BINGEING

Before leaving for the Canadian road trip, Jamie and I had talked about who should take the reins of the book-tour schedule. Jamie, who spends much of life living in fly-by-the-seat-of-your-pants-ville was flabbergasted at the idea that the libraries, schools, cafes and bookshops might need some advance notice of his arrival, but I had an inkling that they would. And so, in a bid to ease any stress during the road trip, I had been appointed as lead tour manager. Or rather, I had appointed myself. I'd taken great care to create a mega Excel spreadsheet, which detailed exactly when and where we needed to be for each week of the tour. It was a sheet that boasted a disgusting amount of colour-coding and was proudly titled 'PLANADA'.

Every decision we made on the journey was, therefore, answerable to one single adventure goddess and her name was Planada. Planada and her technicoloured Excel dream coat would be our guiding light through the darkness of winter. She would make sure we got to all the local venues on time and that no punter was disappointed. Of equal importance, she would also make sure that we had time to explore cool national parks and vibrant cities en route – something that was important to me.

We'd managed to stay on schedule in Newfoundland and the same was true as we motored across Nova Scotia. We were doing so well with the schedule that we even had time to take a side trip to Prince Edward Island and spend an afternoon wandering between snow-covered dunes on Cavendish Beach. But as Jamie, Magster, Monty the Moose and I entered the province of New Brunswick, we were beginning to slip behind. Planada was angry. We needed to make a sacrifice to appease her and get back on her good side pronto, and that meant cracking out a few long days of dawn-to-dusk driving.

We were midway through one of those long days behind the wheel, when we stopped in for lunch with a family in

Grand Falls, New Brunswick. Originally, Heather and her kids had offered to host us for a night. We felt sad about not being able to take them up on their offer but decided that sharing a meal together would come a close second. She fed us thick winter soup, topped with British dumplings and pierogies on the side, and we washed it all down with big mugs of tea.

As we waved goodbye to the family and waddled, full-bellied, back to the car, Heather came running down the snowy driveway behind us. She caught up with us and handed over a bag of satsumas and a box of home-baked cookies. 'We can't have you wasting away out there now, can we?' she smiled.

I was pretty sure that I'd eaten enough food in the past few months to be able to hibernate through winter and still wake up plump, but it was a lovely gesture. And besides, having a box of fruit in the car might go some way towards improving our road-trip eating habits.

We were part way through dishing out a goodbye hug, when Heather said, 'There's snow coming in, you know. Are you sure you don't want to stay?'

I thought for a moment and looked at Jamie. We'd been lucky on the journey so far and had not been held up by any adverse weather. I looked up at the sky – it was clear and blue, without a cloud in it.

'Ah, that's so lovely of you, Heather, but we've really got to make it to Quebec tonight,' Jamie said. 'I've got a talk at a bookstore tomorrow.'

'It's only a few hours' drive. I think we'll be alright,' I added.

'Okay, of course. It's your call. If you hit any trouble, you know where we are,' Heather smiled. 'Just promise me one thing…?'

'What's that?' I asked.

'That you'll be off the road before dark?'

'Promise,' we said.

More goodbye hugs were dished out, taking care not to squash the bag of satsumas in the process and off we went, Magster's winter-studded tyres turning slowly over snow and ice as we rolled out of Grand Falls and set off for Rivière-du-Loup, Quebec.

The first hour of driving was plain sailing and there was no sign of the snow we'd been warned about. But, by the second hour, light flakes had begun drifting down from the sky and now the snow was getting heavier. Jamie was at the wheel, and although his default is to drive at grandad speed, he was now going even more slowly than usual on account of the snowy conditions – at great-grandad speed. The snow continued to get heavier and heavier until I couldn't see the lines on the road at all, or the edge of it for that matter. Worse than that, the few cars that had been on the road had now been replaced by big trucks – articulated lorries that kicked up their own mini blizzards as they passed. Even worse still, we had broken our promise to Heather: because of travelling at great-grandad speed, we'd made slow progress and it was getting dark.

I felt like an idiot. Why hadn't we taken her advice and just stayed put? We could have been safe and warm, snuggled up on Heather's sofa, rather than playing spot the road markings on a snowy highway. *What on earth made us think that we knew more than the locals did about driving in a Canadian winter?* I thought. Then again, as my dad always says, 'We all wish we had a Master's in hindsight, Anna,' and, as foolish as I felt, I knew that dwelling on the coulda woulda shoulda's wouldn't stop the snow from falling. I wrestled my thoughts back to the present.

It was then that I realised that neither one of us had said anything for a good 10 minutes. Jamie was leaning forwards and squinting at the windscreen. I looked ahead at the road. Darkness had fallen fully now and, except for glimpses of the black sky, everything around us was white. In fact, the snow was coming down so thick and so fast that it seemed as if we were moving at light speed, through a galaxy of stars. My heart rate began to rise and adrenaline pulsed through my veins.

'J…' I said, slowly.

'Yep,' he replied, not flinching and keeping his gaze fixed ahead.

'Do you feel safe?'

'No, not really.'

'Me neither… I don't like it. I don't think we should be driving in this.'

'I was thinking the same thing. How far are we from town?' he asked.

'About twenty miles. But there's a motel off the road at the next junction. I think we should pull in and spend the night there.'

'Agreed. Let's do it. Time to get off the road.'

We turned the radio off so that Jamie could concentrate and willed the next exit to appear from the darkness.

'Okay… the junction's coming up soonish. Keep an eye out,' I said.

But in the process of slowing down to make sure we didn't miss the exit, we hadn't noticed that a large lorry had over- taken us on the left-hand side. It cut back into our lane far too quickly and kicked up an almighty wave of snow onto the windscreen.

Everything went white.

'Waaaaaaaa!' I started hyperventilating and we both be- gan screaming.

'I can't see!' Jamie yelled.

'Shiiiiiittttttt!' I hollered back as we continued to drive blindly into a wall of white at 40 mph. My heart was going like the clappers. Five seconds went by. Surely we were going to crash! There was no way we wouldn't crash! Ten seconds passed. Our world was still white and I needed to brace for impact. I shut my eyes and focused on breathing. In. Out. In.

Out. In… I could hear the squeak of the windscreen wipers, working overtime to clear the snow. In. Out. In. Out… Fifteen seconds passed but no impact came. I opened one eye. And then the other. A patch of white had cleared from the windscreen and Jamie was leant forwards, peering through it.

'You okay?' he asked.

'Mm-hmm,' I whimpered.

A large clump of snow dropped from the windscreen and Jamie let out a huge sigh of relief. 'Bloody Nora. That was unbeliev—'

'Oh no! We missed it!' I shouted, putting my head in my hands as I glimpsed the corner of the green exit sign whizz by my side window. That was it. We'd passed the last available place to exit the highway before Rivière-du-Loup. There was nothing for it but to drive on.

Jamie reduced his driving to great-great-great-grandad speed for the remaining miles to the city and I tried to reduce my heart rate, but to no avail. By the time we finally made it off the motorway, it'd been dark for an hour. We'd been on tenterhooks for much of that time and the adrenaline of the truck incident had taken its toll. I was a nervous wreck and Jamie looked as white as our surroundings.

Arriving in the city, I cursed myself yet again – this time for not having booked a place to stay ahead of time. We passed a few small hotels and B&Bs but were horrified to find that the snow was piled up so high out the front of each of them that we wouldn't have been able to park Magster. Her wheels didn't have the greatest grip at the best of times and she was a heavy beast, laden with boxes of Jamie's book and all our gubbins for the journey. If we got her stuck in the snow it would be days before we'd be able to get her out again. Throughout the city, whole cars had been swallowed up in snowdrifts, with only their antennas peeking out from beneath the piles of white, and the streets were deserted. A slow creep of panic began to rise in me... *Where would we go? How would we manage to find somewhere to stay?* I thought.

I couldn't take much more. I needed a distraction, so I opened Heather's box of cookies, which was on my lap, and put one in my mouth. I continued to munch on them as we drove slowly down the main street.

'What do you want to do?' Jamie asked.

'I don't know,' I said, putting another cookie into my mouth. Just then, we passed a large posh-looking hotel. It was lit up like a Christmas tree and through floor-to-ceiling glass windows I could see a gigantic chandelier suspended in the lobby. Most importantly, they had a snow plough out in the car park. Hallelujah! We rolled Magster into the posh car park, parked her on a freshly ploughed parking space and handed over an eye-watering 250 Canadian dollars for a room. It was four times over our budget for the night but, by that point, I didn't care and neither did Jamie.

Safely in our hotel room, with Magster being slowly covered by snow in the car park, we flopped backwards onto the bed and stared at the ceiling. I let out a long breath.

'Oh, my days,' I said, feeling relieved to be somewhere away from the snow.

'What in the world just happened?' said Jamie.

'I'm not sure, J, but let's not do that again,' I replied, turning sideways to look at him on the bed. I could see the relief in his eyes too.

'That was terrifying,' he said, shaking his head.

'It was.' I then realised that I was holding something in my hands. I looked down and started laughing.

'What? What is it?' Jamie asked.

'They're gone.'

'Gone?'

'The cookies! I ate them all,' I said, brandishing an empty cardboard box.

'You what?! But there were twenty of them in there!'

'I know, but I was so stressed, and I just started nibbling and I didn't think and… I ate the whole blooming box!'

Oh yes. In all the madness I had inadvertently consumed a whole box of cookies. Talk about blizzard bingeing. If only I'd had the box of satsumas on my lap instead.

As it turned out, Jamie's event at the bookstore in Rivière-du-Loup was cancelled on account of the poor weather. We spent an extra night in the extortionately priced hotel and vowed to have learned our lesson as we continued the journey west across the country. I had a word with Planada, to let her know that things would be different from then on, and we warned all the book venues that there was a chance that we might not make it on time – because the weather could hold us up. That, or because I was buried under a mound of cookies.

ADOPTED CITIZENS

By the midpoint in our journey – despite our blizzard blunder – we had really settled into life as temporary Canadians. I had learned what a toque is (it's a bobble hat), that kilometres are sometimes called 'clicks' and at precisely which temperature my nostril hair and eyelashes began to freeze (this is −25°C). I'd become addicted to A&W root beer and chicken baskets, as well as steaming bowls of Tim Hortons' chilli – all of which were readily available in most towns. We were even driving like locals too, allowing for long braking distances on the ice and drifting around corners like pros.

One of the greatest lessons, however, was that, in order to make sure the engine would splutter into life, we needed to start the car 15 minutes before intending to leave in the morning. I relished the morning ritual of 'bonnet brushing' and the sick satisfaction that came from scraping the car free of ice. I especially loved kicking the mudflaps on the front wheel and watching a block of slush the size of the Empire State Building drop to the ground. And of course, a few times, I mistakenly believed that I could do all these things without gloves on because 'I went to Scotland once and it was cold there'. The excruciating surge of pain in my fingertips let me know otherwise.

When Christmastime rolled around we were treated to not one, but several family celebrations in homes across Ontario. Socks, gloves, winter boots and a pair of snowshoes were among the gifts, but as the journey wore on, we collected memories that were more precious than anything you could find in a Christmas stocking. With Planada now back on side, we took a side trip to one of the wonders of the natural world: Niagara Falls. And even though it was the third time I'd met Lady Niagara, I still looked out across her cascades and thought *HOW IS THAT EVEN FREAKIN' POSSIBLE?!* It was −20°C and the mist from the falls had been blown onto the trees on the opposite bank, turning each one into a giant icicle and making every scrap of their branches white.

Near the tiny town of Wawa, we were hosted by a local who lived in a large rustic chalet, right on the edge of mighty Lake Superior. We ate blueberry pancakes for breakfast by the fire and took an early morning stroll on the wild and wind-swept shores of the lake. We marvelled at lumps of ice the size of mini footballs, which had washed up onto the grey sand of the beach and resembled scattered crystal balls.

At Thunder Bay, we were taken dog sledding, reveling in a

ride through an evergreen forest under the cover of darkness, staring at the butts of happy huskies and feeling the force of their pull through the trees. Jamie also had his first crack at ice fishing and, despite not catching anything for tea, adored it. Apparently, ice fishing is all about the man-chat bonding and not about the catching of fish anyway.

When we made Winnipeg, or Winterpeg, as it's affectionately known to Canadians, local resident Judy took us skating at The Forks, where the Red and Assiniboine Rivers meet. Both rivers freeze over in the wintertime so that you can skate for miles along them. Well, of course, unless you're Jamie and me, and then you skate and fall over for miles along them instead. All in all, I grew used to the rhythm of a Canadian winter. The mercury dipping into the minus 30s on a daily basis, bundling bags and weary bodies into Magster and hitting the road in search of peach and lilac sunrises over sparkling lakes and frosted forests.

Of all the memories we created that year, there's one day that stands out. It was the day we went hiking in Algonquin National Park, near Ottawa. The nose-tingle-ometer read 'very cold' so we wrapped up warm and packed shortbread and flasks of coffee for a five-hour trek through winter wonderland. It was late morning as we ducked and weaved our way between the evergreens. My shoulders brushed the branches as I passed, disturbing fresh snow that had been taking respite on the outstretched arms of each tree. Pockets of powder dropped to the floor, making the satisfying sound of snow falling onto snow – a soft, almost inaudible 'pfft'. Beyond that was the crunch and squeak of our boots, moving steadily over frozen puddles, branches and long-forgotten pine cones.

With frosted flakes gathering on our eyelashes, and fingers and noses starting to tingle, we pressed on past small waterfalls, frozen mid-cascade over slick black rocks. I stopped for a moment, looking up at the blue sky in the gap between the white-dusted trees and tried to take it all in. We were standing in 2,900 square miles of wilderness and I suspected that we wouldn't see another soul on the hike, a fact which made it all the more special. It was a day that I wanted to pause time on, and walk back and forth through its precious moments. I inhaled a long deep breath and was rewarded with a newfound silence unlike anything I'd experienced before. Despite the biting temperature in the snowy wilderness, that silence soothed me. Within a few hours of us being alone in the park, my head felt clearer.

Sometimes, I forget that much of the noise of life is in our minds. Personally, it's like a rock concert in mine on many days. And beyond lessons about driving in blizzards, starting car engines and learning the correct name for a bobble hat, Canada had taught me one very special thing. That the only sound that can ever truly drown out the unwanted noise in your mind, is the snow-tipped silence of nature.

BROKEN DREAMS ON THE DOWNS

England.
Spring, 2013.

Originally, I'd hoped to use the Easter weekend to cycle the length of the River Thames, following a trail along its banks from the source at Cirencester; in the west, to Southend-on-Sea in the east of England. Unfortunately (and not for the first time) National Rail had scuppered one of life's great escapes by selecting that weekend to cancel all trains to the west. Faced with the prospect of sitting at home in my pants instead of going adventuring, I held an emergency adventure meeting (with myself) and came up with a last-minute plan B. Instead of cycling the length of the Thames on a touring bike, I would mountain bike the South Downs Way. Excited by the idea of getting on a bike with very knobbly tyres, I eagerly loaded up the South Downs Trail website and read the description of the route:

'If you are interested in great views, attractive wildlife, visible prehistory, fine pubs and pretty villages, or if you just fancy a challenge, the South Downs Way awaits you.'

How marvellous. Although 'visible prehistory' sounded more like something from the *Embarrassing Bodies* show on the telly than the English countryside, the pubs, views and the challenge were all right up my street. Plus, if the Downs was 'awaiting' me, it'd be plain rude not to turn up. Now convinced that the trail was the perfect fit for an Easter adventure, I shared the plan B with my good friend and adventure compadre Lydia.

Lydia is one of my favourite people on planet Earth. Not only because of her laid-back attitude and cheery disposition, but because whenever I give her a call with an adventure idea and ask if she'd like to come along, 90% of the time she replies with 'go on then'. The only time she ever turns me down is when she's doing something like trekking with donkeys in Georgia, cycling across Europe or taking time to visit her family in Liverpool. She once even joined me for part of my bike ride through all 50 states of the USA – but that's a whole 'nother story.

I would like to clarify at this point that neither Lydia nor I had ridden a mountain bike for a long time. That wasn't necessarily a problem, but Lydia and I share an affliction. That is, we believe we can do anything someone else can, if we just… try. And so, after reading in our trusty guidebook that 'experienced mountain bikers can do the 100-mile South Downs Trail in two days', we translated this into 'two semi-fit girls, who can't mountain bike, but can sort of ride other things, can do the 100-mile trail in two days'. Which, I'm sure you'll agree, was all very logical.

I met Lydia on Easter Saturday outside a busy Winchester train station. She was easy to spot through the crowd of tourists – a tall, lone figure, her long, dark-brown hair fashioned into a ponytail and a large backpack at her feet, complete with a camping mat strapped to the bottom of it. She was standing next to a white mountain bike which looked like it'd seen better days and she had a look of trepidation on her face.

'Hiya Lyds! You ready to rock?' I said, wheeling my bike from the platform and through the barrier towards her.

'Err, I'm ready to fall off a lot,' She grimaced.

'Oh good. Me too. If we don't fall off, I'll be suing the trail trust for false advertising.'

'I feel like I haven't packed enough stuff though, you know...' Lydia said, hauling her backpack up onto her shoulders.

'I'm sure you'll be fine. Did you remember a bivvy?'

'Yep. I borrowed one. No idea how to use it... It looks like a body bag.'

'Well. Technically it is a body bag... of sorts'

'I suppose. I just hope I don't get claustrophobic in there...' she said.

Side by side, we wheeled our bikes through Winchester and towards the start of the trail on the outskirts of the city. It was a chilly spring morning but the sun was out, beaming through gaps in the surrounding buildings and lighting up the pavement. We passed under the shadow of Winchester Cathedral and marvelled at its intricate stonework and medieval spires which reached into the clouds, before arriving at the first signpost for the South Downs Way. I looked past the sign and noted that the trail began by going up a steep hill.

'Well… no time like the present to test out those granny cog gears,' Lydia chirped, hopping onto her bike and setting off up the climb with me in hot pursuit. By the time we reached the top, I was gasping for breath and could taste blood. One mile down, just 99 to go.

After the first lung-tickling hill, things got easier and I took that as a sign that I needed to shock my body into life – to remind it that, although we were on the Downs for a jolly, it would jolly well have to pull its finger out to make forward progress. The trail continued onwards and upwards, following quiet country lanes and passing through a woodland filled with beech trees. Soon the landscape began to open out and we were streaking along a flatter section, cutting between fields of honey-coloured maize and riding on dusty grey rubble, which stretched out from beneath our wheels and disappeared into the horizon like a set of train tracks.

We kept our legs turning as best we could, chatting in between the ups and downs, crossing the sometimes rolling, sometimes sharp, folds of the English countryside. After an hour of riding, I concluded that I was becoming a dab hand at this mountain-biking malarkey. The flat sections were always a welcome relief, but I actually began to look forward to each uphill effort and the inevitable downhill that followed. I've never been one for enjoying going downhill on a bike – I don't like the lack of control on long descents. But the downhills on the South Downs are brief. Brief enough for me to be able to keep my imagination in check and buckle up for a short, sharp, thrill of a ride. So I took great joy in steaming down the hills, hanging my butt off the back of the saddle, just like I'd seen the pros do on the telly box, and using my bent knees as shock absorbers over the rocks and roots of the trail beneath my wheels.

With all the bouncing and butt-hanging, before long, I began to feel RADICAL. *This is awesome!* I thought. *I* am awesome. In fact, I am a bodacious, cool mountain-biker babe. On one particular descent, I was enjoying myself so much that I had my mouth wide open like a goldfish – whooping and hollering – lost in the wonderment of it all. Just then, the bike hit a large clump of what looked like dried mud. The mud got swept up by the front wheel and, with no mudguards to disturb its upwards trajectory, the clump was released from the wheel and flew skyward, into my mouth. It hit my tongue and bounced out of my mouth again, leaving behind a faint taste of sheep faeces.

When not engaged in a battle with mud, gravel, poop or steep hills, I could look up and out on the Hampshire countryside, which often resembled a patchwork quilt. Oddly shaped squares of light green and golden brown were stitched together by thick green-black hedgerows and lines of trees. Much as I loved the dramatic landscapes of places like South America, the USA and New Zealand, there was something about the rolling hills of England that would always be dear to my heart. It was a landscape that was less impressive, but that made it seem more welcoming too. As if the greens and the browns were beckoning us to ride on through.

By mid-afternoon Lydia and I had covered 25 miles. To celebrate making one quarter of the total length of the trail we stopped at the visitor centre cafe in Queen Elizabeth Country Park. The first thing that struck me as I stepped off the bike was how hungry I was. I'd had a gigantic breakfast before leaving home, then a second one on the train but, pulling in at the visitor centre, I was ravenous. Being a Saturday afternoon, the cafe was busy so we sat down for lunch amid a backdrop of excited chatter, the clinking of cutlery and clatter of china plates. I ordered a cheese and ham panini with a side of ready salted crisps (which I put in the panini, of course) and then washed it all down with a chocolate milkshake, a banana and two apples. Lydia enjoyed a similar mini feast and, fully refuelled, we hit the trail again.

The cafe was in a dip of land surrounded by dense forest, so we climbed upwards through dappled sunlight, wheels turning over a reddish-brown carpet of fallen beech leaves. The further we moved away from the bustle of the visitor centre, the more we could hear the wind rustling through the tree canopy above our heads. Strong gusts freed leaves from branches, leaves which showered down on us like confetti and settled on our arms and shoulders as we pedalled.

In spite of the beautiful surroundings, it wasn't long after leaving the visitor centre – an hour or so – that my energy began to dip. My eyelids grew heavy, my legs felt leaden and, even though it was a cold afternoon, I would happily have curled up at the side of the trail and drifted off to sleep under a bush. Of course, instead of attributing this to a lack of fitness, I blamed the panini. All that white bread had shot my sugar levels up and now I was crashing. We reached a junction between two recently ploughed fields and pulled the bikes to a stop.

'Lyds... How are you feeling?' I asked, looking down at my handlebars and trying to act as if it was a casual enquiry.

'Me? I'm pretty tired,' she sighed.

'You are? Phew. Me too. We've got some options here though,' I said, looking at the map. 'We can crack on for another fifteen miles... and that'll take us to fifty miles for the day...'

'Or...?' Lyds asked.

'Or, we could find somewhere nearby to camp for the night.'

There was a moment of silence as Lydia looked down the trail ahead.

'What time is it?' she asked.

'Err... five p.m.'

'Hmm... it's a bit early to camp, isn't it?'

'It is... But if we take a left up there, there's a tiny village with a pub... so we could have a hot dinner then find a field nearby to sleep in and—'

'There's a pub?!' Lydia's eyes lit up.

'Yep,' I grinned.

'Well, why didn't you say that in the first place? Stuff it. We'll make up the miles tomorrow. Let's go.'

And so, we detoured a few miles from the South Downs Way to enjoy some pub grub at the spectacularly named Unicorn Inn in Heyshott. I was hoping to be able to order rainbows and stardust for dinner but, as that wasn't an option (perhaps it was out of season), I ordered a bowl of Cumberland sausages with buttery mashed potato, loaded with gravy and caramelised onions instead. Lydia chose a winter vegetable stew, topped with sticky dumplings, and we both had steamed sponge pudding for afters, which was drowning in treacle – just as it should be. We followed all of that with two Whisky Macs and, although I don't like whisky, I discovered that, when combined with ginger wine (which I love), the drink reminded me of Christmas and was surprisingly delicious.

Stuffed with pub fare, we stepped out into the crisp night air at 10 p.m. The moon was high in the sky and the temperature had dropped dramatically during the hours we'd spent by the fire inside. We didn't waste any time in hopping on the bikes and pedalling off up the lane in search of a field to sleep in for the night.

After riding for 10 minutes, we found a suitably secluded sleeping spot in the corner of a field. I piled on everything I had in my backpack – three thermal tops, a gilet, two pairs of socks, three sets of bottoms and a hat – and felt like the Michelin Man as I clambered into a four-seasons sleeping bag and shimmied into my bivvy bag.

'Thanks for the night out at the local,' said Lydia, zipping herself into her sleep cocoon.

'Always a pleasure,' I replied.

'Night Anna.'

'Night Lyds. Sleep well.'

I lay awake for 30 minutes, enjoying a tickle of cool night air across my nose, looking up at a blanket of stars and watching clouds drift in front of a cream-coloured full moon.

At 3 a.m. I woke up and realised I needed a pee. The moon had turned pearly white and was now shining so brightly that I didn't need my torch to find a quiet corner of the frosty field and release my Whisky Mac. Post whisky-wee, I wriggled back into my bag and heard a noise from where Lydia was sleeping, a few metres away. It sounded like sharp intakes of breath. She had zipped fully into her bivvy bag so I couldn't see her face, but I could tell by watching the material of the bag that her body was shaking.

'Lyds… Lydia? Are you okay?'

'Y-yeaahhh,' came her stuttered reply.

'Are you sure?' I asked.

'I'm… okay… I'm jus-st a b-b-it cold, that's all,' she stammered.

'Oh crikey. Have you got any more clothes to put on?'

'N-n-no, I'm wearing them all.'

'Have you managed to get any sleep?' I asked.

'N-n-n-not yet.'

'Oh Lyds!'

'I kn-now… I told you I should have packed more… I'll b-be okay. The d-d-dumplings are keeping me warm,' she joked.

'I could take a layer off and give it to you?' I said.

'N-no-no… you're alright. I'm getting comfy now. I'm s-s-sure I'll sleep soon…'

The weather app on my phone told me that it was −6°C, which was unseasonably cold for the middle of spring, so I could see why Lydia had been caught off guard. I was only staying warm thanks to clothes that I'd thrown into my bag 'just in case'. And besides, ordinarily at this time of year, we'd be snuggled up, waiting for a visit from the Easter Bunny, in warm, cosy beds – not laid out like frozen slugs in a field in Heyshott. After Lydia assured me again that she'd be alright, I settled back into my own bag to sleep. I could still hear her chattering teeth as I drifted off and was genuinely concerned that I'd wake up to find that she had hypothermia.

When daybreak arrived, I was delighted to discover that Lydia was alive and well. She croaked a good morning from inside her bivvy and announced that she'd had a 'solid nap' sometime around 4 a.m. Even though I'd managed to get a decent amount of sleep, I was feeling groggy as we set about packing up camp and preparing to get back on the South Downs Trail. I was keen to get my legs turning and some blood pumping back around my body.

'Fancy a Toffee Crisp?!' Lydia shouted as she stuffed the last few things back into her backpack. I looked over to see her holding two chocolate bars in bright-orange packets.

'Where have you been hiding those?!' I gasped.

'Ah, in my secret stash. I always carry a Toffee Crisp… for emergencies, you know?' she grinned.

We both agreed that a sleepless night and a chilly morning were quite the emergency, so I snatched a Toffee Crisp and proclaimed it a pre-breakfast treat. Having spent a night chilling in the Heyshott freezer, the bars were definitely more crisp than toffee, but they did the trick of perking us up as we crowbarred our feet into our stiff, ice-encrusted cycling shoes and wheeled the bikes back to the road. We clambered onto our saddles, primed and ready for another day of highs, lows and everything in between, and each let out a cheer as we took the first few pedal strokes. Three revolutions of the wheels later and I heard… 'CRUNCH!'

'Err, Anna?'

'Yep!' I called over my shoulder.

'My bike's not well,' Lydia wailed.

Unfortunately, the frosty weather had upset Lydia's steed. Her rear chain cassette had given up the ghost. If she tried to pedal, it just spun round and round. The cold had stiffened up the grease in the magic freehub, which helps the cassette to grip onto and propel the wheel forwards so, when she pedalled, the cassette spun freely, getting her nowhere fast. I couldn't help but laugh as I hung my head between my hands over my handlebars and let out a deep sigh.

Neither of us was a bike mechanic, but we suspected that there was no easy fix for Lydia's bike. It would need taking apart and some expert 'fiddling' – both of which we didn't have the tools for. Perhaps we should have packed emergency tools instead of Toffee Crisps. Being Easter Sunday, there were no buses running that early in the morning (and I'm not sure we'd have been able to get our bikes onto them if they were). There was nothing for it but to begin a 12-mile walk to the nearest train station at Haslemere. It was a Sunday stroll that wasn't easy in stiff-soled, partially frozen cycling shoes, but it turned out to be one of the most enjoyable parts of the whole South Downs extravaganza. The air was crisp, there wasn't a soul on the streets and the sun was shining brightly for the first time in weeks. It was a sublime day to be out and about in the countryside.

After travelling a total of 50 miles – 38 miles of cycling and 12 miles of hobbled hiking with bikes – we bundled our weary bodies onto the train at Haslemere and headed back to London. I found great comfort in being able to feel my toes again for the first time since leaving the Unicorn Inn and took a moment to reflect on how the adventure plan B had panned out. We'd set out to ride the length of the South Downs Way but had instead bookended a 38-mile cycle with on-bike body shock and a dose of mild hypothermia. I felt a tinge of embarrassment at having not completed the full distance, more because we'd been so naive in believing that we could. But I was too tired to care and resolved that we'd just have to come back to the trail another time (with extra Toffee Crisps). Truth be told, we'd embarked on and engaged willingly in a complete shambles – one which had strayed so wonderfully off-piste from first intentions that it was barely recognisable. It wasn't the first time *that* had happened and I had an inkling it wouldn't be the last. With the Surrey countryside whizzing past the window, Lydia and I allowed the warmth of the carriage and the gentle rocking of the train tracks to send us into a deep sleep. We rested our heads against the glass and nodded and dribbled – carried through our slumber back towards our normal, sensible lives.

COAST TO COAST

New Zealand.
Kiwi summer, 2018.

I'm standing on Kumara Beach on the west coast of New Zealand's South Island. Dawn is breaking and the sun, a gentle giant orb, creeps ever so slowly above blackened hills beyond the dunes. Patches of peach glow in a cornflower-blue sky and faint wisps of cloud drift above the sand, some grey, some white – gently fusing and dispersing, as if they too are taking their sweet time to wake up and greet the day.

Standing next to me is my good friend Hollie, and we're wearing matching kit: black shorts and green and white cycling jerseys, with race bibs pulled over the top that proudly display our team number, 774. As we crouch down to put our hands in the waters of the Tasman Sea I feel a flutter of nerves in my belly. It's like a swarm of butterflies taking flight and enough to make me want to throw up my breakfast. I look at Hollie and she smiles. 'You ready, McNuff?' she asks.

'Ready,' I say, exhaling a long breath. 'Let's do this.'

DAY ONE:
THE PAIN CAVE

New Zealand's Coast to Coast race is a multisport adventure which takes place in the land of the long white cloud in February each year. It sees endurance enthusiasts run, cycle and kayak 152 miles across the rugged landscapes of the South Island, from the Tasman Sea to the Pacific Ocean.

Many hard-as-nails athletes do the whole shebang in a single day but I fancied making the journey through the stunning landscape of New Zealand a more leisurely affair. So I'd chosen to join forces with seasoned pocket-rocket and Kiwi native Hollie Woodhouse, to complete the course over two days, as a team. Hollie and I had been friends ever since she spent some time living in London, a few years back. A mutual friend had introduced us and we'd then put the world to rights over a burrito – a solid foundation for any relationship, if you ask me. So solid in fact that Hollie allowed me to move in with her in Christchurch a few months prior to the event. We spent mornings paddling on the Avon River, evenings running in the hills and the weekends doing recces to complete sections of the course at a more leisurely pace.

Even though Hollie had done the Coast to Coast race twice before, she'd never completed it as part of a duo so it would be a new experience for her too. I had no idea what to expect but I had read that success in the event relies on having a good 'support team' – people who would ferry our bikes between stages and lay out all our food and clothing so that we could move swiftly between running, cycling and kay-aking. Every second spent on the course counted towards our overall position and if the time it took me to find a matching pair of socks at home was anything to go by, we'd need all the help we could get.

Fortunately, with our stellar support crew, composed of seven friends and family members (including my parents who just *happened* to be on holiday in New Zealand at the time), we were in with a chance of keeping up with the best of them. And if we could sneak ourselves a space on the tandem-team podium come the end of those two days, I'd return home to the UK one very happy bunny.

They say that getting to the start line of an adventure is half of the battle, and that was especially true for team 774. First of all, we narrowly avoided destroying our bikes the night before the race, when we drove into the carport of our rented house with them strapped on the top of the car, nearly crush-ing them against the roof. And second of all, despite a 5 a.m. wake-up on race day, Hollie and I managed to break the Guin-ness World Record for fannying around. Cue leaving the house late, getting stuck in a traffic jam of race supporters, a frantic scrabble to drop our bikes at the transition area and a sprint down to the start on Kumara Beach. Nothing like adding a few extra miles of lung-busting running to a 152-mile trans-coun-try adventure.

Thankfully, our start wave was delayed (I can only assume that the organisers were fannying around too), so Hollie had time to test out the pre-race Portaloo facilities, which she rated at a solid 8/10. As the amber light of dawn cast rays across the faces of a crowd of chattering competitors, we completed our ceremonial hand dip in the Tasman Sea and took our place alongside the other two-day teams at the start line.

'Thirty seconds…' the announcer's voice boomed over the tannoy…

'Feeling good, McNuff?' Hollie asked.

'Feelin' FINE, Woodhouse,' I replied, and it was true.

'Fifteen seconds… Ten seconds… Five… Four… Three… Two… One…'

An air horn sliced through the still morning air and we were on our way! On a journey across New Zealand, bound for the Pacific Ocean.

As we pounded up the sandy trail away from the beach, the adrenaline coursing through my veins was intoxicating. Surrounded by a competitor stampede, I could hear the thunder of trainer hooves moving over soft ground and the odd word being panted or puffed between teammates. Hollie and I did our best to stay together, bobbing and weaving through the crowd, sometimes being overtaken, sometimes pushing on. *Take it easy, Anna. Take it easy. There's a long way to go yet*, said the voice in my head as we continued on up the shallow slope towards the main road.

The first half-mile run passed in a flash and soon we were at the bike transition pen, moving as fast as we could through a sea of wheels, bodies and cycling helmets to reach our steeds. We grabbed them from their racks, hopped into the saddles and heard a satisfying 'bleep!' as we cycled over the first timing chip mat. We were on our way for a 34-mile cycling stage.

The start of the ride went well. My lungs were on fire from having gotten overexcited on the initial run up from the beach and I knew I'd pushed too hard, so I did all I could to deliberately calm my breathing as I took up a race position on the bike, tucked in close behind Hollie as we steamed up the road. In a tactical move, we chose to nestle ourselves in the middle of a 30-strong group of mostly male cyclists, using them as shelter from the wind to help us to conserve precious energy for the miles ahead.

The sun had now risen fully and it lit up a road which passed between granite mountains and patches of dense forest. It was set to be a warm weekend, but the air was still cool as we forged on through rags of morning mist and started up the first climb of the day. Despite being in a race, riding in a group of fellow competitors felt strangely peaceful. Very little was being said – there were only the sounds of gears shifting, chains whirring and the whoosh of air passing through a wave of wheels. Soothed by the relative silence, I managed to keep up the calm breathing and settled into the zone – a magical place where time seems to stand still but the miles pass quickly.

At the 10-mile marker, I watched a cyclist in front of me

take a cereal bar out of his jersey back pocket to eat. *Ah yes. I should have something to eat soon too*, I thought. It had been a few hours since our breakfast at base camp, after all, and I'd already expended more energy than planned in the start-line excitement.

I contemplated my options for a snack and settled on raspberry chocolate logs. These are tubes of tangy raspberry-flavoured liquorice filled with solid lumps of milk chocolate and, second only to pineapple lumps, they are my favourite Kiwi delight. As I reached into my jersey for the logs, it dawned on me. I couldn't remember actually putting any food in my pockets. Did I? I mean, we'd had all our food so neatly laid out on the living room floor, I definitely remember setting aside food for the other race stages and sending it off with the support crew but… *Anna, you idiot!* I thought. *How could you forget your food for the bike ride?!*

In the midst of grappling with my stupidity, I realised I had two choices. I could back off, fess up about my faux pas to Hollie and take things steady or… I could cling on for dear life to this fast-moving group of cyclists in front of me and hope that they would drag me along for the remaining 24 miles to the mountain-run stage.

I went for the death or glory option and, with nothing to fuel my tiring muscles, I began to slip, one pedal stroke at a time, into a bicycle-shaped pain cave. My legs seemed to be moving in slow motion and it felt as if my brakes were jammed on. Everything was heavy. Even holding my head up became an effort. I gripped the handlebars tighter and pressed harder on the pedals, but the more I pushed, the slower I went. I dropped further and further back in the group, until I was the last rider in the 30-strong peloton and clinging on by the skin of my teeth. Hollie had done a cracking job of keeping tabs on where I was and had moved back down the line of riders too. She appeared alongside me and eyed me closely. 'You good, McNuff?' I couldn't hide the grimace on my face, nor could I speak to her, and she sensed something was up. I gave a prompt nod and kept my eyes fixed firmly ahead. If I could just stay in touch with the pack, then all of this was still salvageable. I turned my attention to the tyre on the bike in front of me, gritted my teeth and shoved even harder on the pedals.

By the time we made it to the transition for the mountain run, I was a wobbly mess. I stepped off the bike and ran with it down a rubble trail, onto a grassy area lined with team support crews. 'McNuff needs food!' Hollie yelled as we neared our crew, and she was right.

Soon there were arms coming at me from every direction, getting me out of my cycling shoes, unclipping my helmet. My mum was yanking my leg and putting it in a running trainer, while support team leader Jax handed me fistfuls of the long-awaited raspberry chocolate logs. I crammed them into my mouth, took an emergency banana from my dad and threw on a small running backpack. It was a slick operation. We were fed, dressed and out of transition in under two minutes. I was now ready (or as ready as I could be) for the final stage of the day – a 20-mile run up and over the mountain at Goat Pass.

Now, I'm not sure if you've ever run out of beans on a long ride, run or even a walk. But if you have, you'll know exactly where I was at as we left that transition area. There are many different terms for the pickle I'd gotten myself into. Some call it 'hitting the wall', but by far my favourite description is the term 'bonking'. And oh my, how I had bonked. I was a bonk monster. Bonkzilla, in fact – larger than life, unsteady on my feet and on a rampage through the Kiwi wilds. My legs were jelly, my lungs were on fire again and I could barely walk, let alone run. I could taste blood in my mouth, my fingers had started to tingle (a side effect of lactic acid build-up) and my hands were shaking. I was also slurring my words – something I could see concerned Hollie every time I spoke. I'd pushed myself to this kind of exhaustion before, but only ever at the end of a race. I'd never tried to recover from an energy bonk *while* running 20 miles over a mountain.

I decided to clear the fog on my brain by thinking ahead, so I began running through directions for the next section of the course in my mind, hoping that breaking things down would keep me focused and distract me from just how dreadful I felt. 'Over the swing bridge across the Otira River... Along the light trail through the forest, out onto the riverbed... River crossing number one...' I repeated the words as I followed Hollie up the valley, all the while still cramming food into my mouth and drinking water because, short of stopping and laying down, those were the only two things that were going to bring me back to the land of the living.

An hour or so later, I'd eaten all my snacks and used up

my sickly energy gels, but I was still struggling. We'd been repeatedly overtaken by other teams and solo competitors since leaving the transition area and now I was frustrated. Worse than that, I was embarrassed. I felt like I had let Hollie down. I had let my parents down. I had let her parents down. There everyone was, ploughing time and energy into supporting this race and, because of my lack of attention to detail, I had ballsed it all up. On top of that, I was annoyed at myself. But I also knew that being annoyed was using up *even* more energy, which only led me to feeling more irritated. It was a tornado of self-destruction and I was spinning out of control. At one river crossing, Hollie stopped and waited for me to catch up.

'I'm so sorry, Hollie. I really am,' I said, shaking my head, feeling like we were now moving at such a snail's pace because I just couldn't go any faster.

'No, McNuff! There are no apologies today. We are a team!' she said sternly.

And that was all I needed to snap me out of my funk. Hollie was right. We were a team, and that meant that all triumphs and blunders were shared. Thank goodness for the sensible half of team 774.

I was quiet over the two hours that followed as we climbed steadily up the valley, concentrating on grappling with the demons of the Deception River as we criss-crossed back and forth over the multiple braids of the river as it meandered up the valley, navigating loose rocks and scrambling through the forest that lined the banks on either side. It was a hot day and the cool glacial water felt wonderful on my tired feet. It was even better when the river crossing was up to my waist because I got a full mid-run ice bath. 'Just keep moving. Just keep moving,' I told my legs, doing my best to keep up with Hollie, who was busy making savvy route choices so that we could leapfrog other groups of runners. In Coast to Coast, there's no one set trail to take from the valley floor to the top of the mountain pass – it's a case of 'the top is thataway – off you go'. So when other competitors chose to take what looked like a 'shorter' route across the uneven and rocky riverbed, Hollie would lead us up onto the bank and into the forest. That meant we could move steadily over flatter ground, ultimately saving us energy and allowing for faster progress.

Despite my suffering, I was spurred on by the fact that we were now passing people on the mountain. We'd just overtaken a woman with dark hair and a British flag next to her race number when I heard her shout.

'You're Anna McNuff! I follow you on Instagram!' I spun around to see her grinning.

'I am indeed!' I replied. Although I didn't exactly feel much like myself at that moment in time.

'It's your fault I'm doing this thing, you know,' the woman said.

'It is?!'

'Yep. I read your running book about how amazing New Zealand is… and, well, here I am!'

Oh crikey, I thought. *What had I got the poor woman into?*

'Are you enjoying it… the race I mean?' I asked.

'I am loving it!' she yelled.

'In that case, I take full responsibility,' I smiled.

Whether it was the good vibes from the fellow Brit or the copious amounts of banana and raspberry chocolate in my system, I will never know, but close to the top of the 1,000-metre pass I finally began to feel human again. I had spent a long time in the dank depths of the hurt locker and it was time to crawl back out into the sunshine.

We were now in the upper part of Deception Valley, surrounded by steep grey-banked cliffs, ducking in and out of lush green forest with a crystal-clear river tumbling over rocks down the middle. It was like being on the set of a shampoo advert. Pressing onwards, we crested the top of Goat Pass, doffed our hats to the wooden wilderness hut up there and began tanking it down the other side of the mountain.

I was now on top of the world in every sense – sucking in lungfuls of fresh mountain air as I stretched out my legs, moving faster and faster through tufts of greenish yellow grass which was poking out from dusty orange earth.

'Annnnd she's back!' Hollie shouted, upon seeing my turn of speed.

'And she's wild!' I hollered over my shoulder.

We'd left Deception Valley behind and were now following

the downstream path of another river, the Mingha, weaving through the beech forest along its bank. I looked at the ground beneath my feet, which was coated with beech leaves, scattered like brown-red confetti over the dark, damp earth. Where the ground was too soggy, wooden boardwalk had been laid, and I took great joy in bounding over each section of it, whooping when the boards flexed beneath me and propelled me onwards and upwards like a mini trampoline.

After a quick scramble over a spider's web of tree roots, the valley opened out once again and we now had just 6 miles left to go of the first day of racing. I took a moment to appreciate the colours on this side of the valley, which were gorgeous. The light grey of the pebbles on the riverbed, the aquamarine of the water, the kaleidoscope of greens on the trees lining the bank and, beyond that, towards the finish line, I could see a sea of wild lupins set among tall grass – lilac and blue, tall and proud, swaying in the breeze, waving us on.

A few miles later, Hollie called from behind me: 'You see that, McNuff? You see it?!' I looked to my left. The course was about to take a sharp turn and I could see a crowd gathered a mile or so ahead. I remembered this section from our weekend recce runs, so I knew only too well what came next: it was the final challenge of the day – a mile-long *Riverdance* of destruction over loose pebbles to the finish line. I tried with all my might to move my feet fast like a ninja, but my legs were S.P.E.N.T. I was stumbling around on the rocks like a drunkard, and it felt as if someone had slipped weights into the soles of my shoes. Just as I began to wonder whether it was possible to move any slower, I heard our support crew. 'GO ON, HOL-LIE! GO ON, ANNA! GO ON, TEAM 774!' It was enough to put a lump in my throat and a fire in my belly – we were almost there. One final scramble up the grassy bank away from the river and into the finishers' chute. I grabbed Hollie's hand as the inflatable green Coast to Coast archway came into view. After 7 hours and 47 minutes of racing and a journey to the depths of despair and back, we raised our arms and crossed the finish line on day one of the Coast to Coast.

****

That evening, when I was able to have a coherent conversation again, we joined our support crew to wolf down a hearty Kiwi barbeque, cooked up in the early evening sun by Hollie's mum on the stove of their camper van. As much as I was fond of Hollie, I adored her parents too – I'd visited them a number of times and even spent one afternoon, when I was poorly, curled up on their living room sofa, drifting in and out of sleep, watching Sandra Bullock movies while they fed me bacon and egg pie. As Hollie's family runs a farm, there was a lot of meat action going on at the barbie, so my mum, who's a vegetarian, had nipped off to source herself an alternative dinner. Thirty minutes later she came running over to the camper van with an excited look on her face.

'Anna! Hollie! Do you know where you are?' she asked.

'Err? Yes. I'm at Klondyke Corner. Here. With you,' I said, thinking that my mum was checking in on my sanity after a day of delirium.

'No, no! Where you are in the race!' I realised that, after what had seemed like a disastrous day, I hadn't paid any attention to where we might be in the overall team standings.

'No… But I'm guessing it's last?' I laughed.

'Fourth! You're in fourth. You're twenty minutes behind third place. Think you can make that up on tomorrow's kayak down the gorge?' she asked.

Hollie and I looked at one another.

'I'm not sure, Mum. We'll see,' I said dismissively, taking another mouthful of dinner.

DAY TWO:
SOGGY SARNIES IN THE SHALLOWS

It was 5.30 a.m. the following morning and I was locked in one of the greatest battles known to humankind – the battle between brain and bladder. I was so cosy and comfortable, snuggled deep into my down sleeping bag at the campsite at Klondyke Corner. Hollie and her boyfriend were snoring away at the other end of the tent and I was trying to fall back to sleep. It was no good. I needed to pee. I poked my head out of the tent and saw that the sun was just beginning to rise, spreading an ethereal haze across a sea of long grass as the morning mist lingering in the valley collided with the dawn light. Beyond the campsite, stray honey-coloured sunbeams were hitting the tips of the surrounding mountain peaks, making patches of the grey rock glow gold.

Post Portaloo pee, I busied myself preparing for the day ahead and, by 7 a.m., everyone in the neighbouring tents was awake. Our support crew left the campsite to travel ahead to the first transition point and Hollie and I began cooking up brekkie on the camper van stove. My body was quick to remind me that I'd cycled a long way and run over a mountain the day before but, overall, I felt positive about the day ahead. Having covered 56 miles already, we now had just 97 miles left of our Coast to Coast journey to the Pacific Ocean. We'd kickstart the day with a 10-mile pedal, follow it with 43 miles of kayaking and wind up with 45 more miles of cycling – all of which would lead us to the finish line at New Brighton Beach in Christchurch.

Despite feeling tip-top and confident about the miles to come, I wanted to make doubly sure that everything went smoothly. So, while I was crumbling ginger nut biscuits into my morning porridge, I made a bold decision.

'Woodhouse,' I said.

'Yup, McNuff?' she asked.

'I'm going to swap my timing chip to the other ankle. It didn't go so well yesterday with it on the right leg. So, I think if I put it on the left leg, things will be better.' There was a brief silence during which I wondered whether Hollie was going to tell me I was a fool to believe in such superstitions.

'I like your thinking – I'll swap mine too,' she said.

At 8 a.m., full of coffee, ginger nut biscuits and porridge, the starter air horn blared again and we were off for round deux of the Coast to Coast extravaganza. I wasn't sure if it was because we were now in a time-adjusted start wave and only surrounded by athletes who had gone a similar speed as us on the previous day, or because I knew that I had an emergency stash of ginger nut biscuits in my back pocket but, the second we crossed the start line, I felt in control. I could move easily back and forth through the 20-strong peloton of riders, and even take turns at the front to help speed our progress up the road.

After 10 minutes, I was feeling comfortable… too comfortable, in fact, and I had this nagging feeling that the pace was too slow. I was midway through questioning whether or not to push on, when I noticed the bib numbers on two girls in front of me. They were the tandem team in third place! I glanced at Hollie who was riding next to me, and she'd clocked it too.

'I'm going to overtake…' I whispered.

'Yes, McNuff! DO IT!' she whispered back.

Pressing harder on the pedals, Hollie and I stretched a few

wheel lengths out in front of the group. We followed the road as it snaked around a couple of bends and whooshed down a short hill. I half-expected the rest of the riders to follow our increase in speed but, after a few minutes, we looked back to find that we were alone. No one had made the break with us. That felt good! Hollie flashed me a big grin.

'Nice one, McNuff,' she said.

'Why, thank you,' I replied, and I couldn't help but let my mind drift, if only briefly, to the fact that we were now in with a chance of making it onto the podium. Although we'd need to finish at least nine minutes ahead of the girls we'd just passed to make up the time we'd lost to them yesterday, and there was a long way to go yet.

We finished up the bike stage at Mount White Bridge and prepared to transition to a kayak. As we wheeled our bikes down the bridge ramp and onto the rocky riverbed, we were greeted by a scene that was in stark contrast to our solitary ride on the road – it was an explosion of activity, colour and sound. There were 50 kayaks lined up along the shore and a huge crowd of people – a mix of support crew members, competitors at various stages of race transition and high-vis-clad event officials. I could hear safety announcements being made over megaphones; cheers and claps filled the air; and there was even a helicopter hovering overhead. Somehow above the din I heard our support crew: 'Hollie! Anna! Over here! Well done, girls! Well done!' they shouted.

The support crew did a stellar job of getting us dressed

like two action-woman dolls, helping us shimmy into black neoprene spray skirts, pulling life jackets over our heads and plonking a blue helmet on each of our noggins, before we leapt into Big Bertha the Barracuda (as we had named our yellow kayak) and pushed off from the shore.

There was a satisfying scraping noise and then a 'sssssh' as the boat lost contact with the riverbed and we floated out onto the water. I took a moment to look down the Waimaka-riri River ahead. Fragments of sunlight danced across its tur-quoise surface as it snaked down the valley between green-grey mountains and disappeared into the distance. As we took those first few paddle strokes, I was overcome with excitement. It might seem natural to feel that way at the start of a journey down a river gorge in New Zealand, but I knew that being able to relax enough to feel excited was a luxury. The kayak section of the race was the discipline I'd been the most nervous about. Largely because, at the time of signing up, I had zero kayaking experience.

The course down the Waimakariri (or 'Waimak' to the lo-cals) is renowned for catching out novices like me. The best way to describe the river is like a rope with two frayed ends. At the start and the end of the 45-mile segment are calmer stretches where the river splits into multiple channels. In be-tween those two calmer, braided sections, the water converg-es into one thundering blue mass, forced through a narrow, steep-sided gorge, which creates sets of challenging rapids.

Thankfully, Hollie brought some much-needed experience

to the kayak party, but I'd managed to up my skill level with a guided tester trip down the Waimak a few months earlier. It was a trip that took my kayaking knowledge from zero to hero in just one day, and as an added bonus, I expanded my on-water vocabulary, learning terms like 'wave train' – a train which consists of multiple small waves (which is, sadly, not like the *Orient Express* and does not involve a fine-dining experience); 'rock garden' – an assortment of submerged boulders, just beneath the river surface; and 'boyle' – a mini whirlpool on the river surface which will spin your kayak round, round like a record, baby, if you're not careful. I had also learned when to use the Kiwi term 'sweet as' (although I suspected that this was not kayak-specific).

Thanks to that trip, and to an extra on-water recce in a jet boat a few weeks later, when Hollie and I pushed away from the crowds on the bank on race day, I was less worried about falling in and more concerned with enjoying the wild ride. Hollie was up the front of the boat, in charge of the steering, and I was in the back, in charge of paddling like heck and dishing out team morale. We settled into a familiar rhythm – our paddles moving in sweet synchronicity through the glacial water, as we swung our bodies from left to right, leaving behind small white-water puddles as we meandered down the valley.

Sadly, the meditative state didn't last long. It turned out to be drama a-go-go in the first hour as we dodged between kayaks getting spun backwards on rocks that were usually deep below the surface but were now exposed, thanks to a lower water level.

'This is the lowest I've ever seen it!' Hollie shouted as we narrowly avoided a surprise boulder ourselves. Some sections were so shallow that Big Bertha got beached on a shoal. Hollie and I realised that, in order to progress, we would have to bum-shuffle the boat forwards. Teamwork made the dream work as we unleashed vigorous, well-timed forward-thrusting hip movements that would have made any Salsa dancer proud.

Soon, we came upon a section of the course that looked familiar from our recce trips, and I noticed that the river had started to deepen and increase in flow.

'Is that the start of the gorge?' I shouted.

'Yup!' Hollie shouted back, and my stomach flipped a mini somersault.

The gorge was a gateway to another world. The day was now hotting up and the sun was shining brightly, so the ordinarily blue river appeared more aquamarine than I'd ever seen it. Granite bluffs shot up from the water, reaching for the clouds as I craned my neck to catch a glimpse of their tops. Small, scraggy trees and green bushes clung to the rock face in places, gravity pulling their lower branches so close to the water that it appeared as if they were dripping into it.

But Mother Nature was quick to remind us that we weren't there to enjoy the scenery, and she soon slapped us with the business end of the rapids. Suddenly, there was a shout from Hollie – 'Paddle, paddle, paddle!' – as our yellow kayak entered what looked like the inside of a washing machine. Moments later, we were engulfed by swirling glacial water –

water I could have sworn was blue just a moment ago, but now all I could see was foaming white. I dug in to follow Hollie's command, moving my arms like a windmill and, after a few seconds, we popped out the other side of the foam and into clear water.

'Wahoo!' I hollered. My heart was pounding, my hands were shaking and I was full to the brim with adrenaline. What a day to be alive!

For the next two hours, we flitted between watching other kayakers fall out of their kayaks and wondering whether we were about to. There were several occasions when our kayak was tipped over at such an angle in front of me that one side of Hollie's entire torso was in the water, but, somehow, we still managed not to tip in. On another occasion, we ended up so close to a bluff that we abandoned the use of our paddles entirely and dragged ourselves along the rock with our hands, cutting my arm in the process. Nothing like a little blood and rock hugging on your way down the Waimakariri to spread the love. We were living life from one swirling corner to the next and loving it.

One of the joys of being in a tandem kayak is that you can take turns to eat and drink. We did this often in between the rapids, sampling the delights of a chocolate brownie-flavoured energy bar (which took an eternity to chew and swallow), some readily accessible raspberry chocco logs (all hail the logs!) and bite-sized pieces of cheese and marmite sandwiches – which I had gone to great lengths to stash in a ziplock bag. Only, somehow, the water had gotten into the bag and what once were sandwiches were now a floating, congealed mess. With no spare food on hand, I went full-blown feral adventure racer, clawing at handfuls of wet white bread and stuffing it into my pie hole.

By the fourth hour, and on account of passing through wave trains that were the size of small houses, our boat had begun to take on water – something that wasn't being helped by the fact that our spray skirts, which were supposed to keep the water out, were letting water in. And… if I'm being really honest, the liquid levels in our boat probably weren't helped by the fact that I had had five wees since leaving the transition area. I know! Five wees while kayaking! I was very proud of myself. Being able to piddle while paddling was quite the accomplishment.

Come the exit of the gorge, just as the river began to open out again and the steep sides dropped away, the kayak felt like a tank and our energy levels were beginning to wane. I knew that we could do with emptying the kayak out, but we didn't want to waste time stopping at the bank to do it. Who knew where those girls in third place were, after all. They could be right behind us. Just then, as if by magic, the decision was made for us. At the last possible rapid we could fall in, we tipped!

'Waaaaaaa!' I yelped, slipping sideways into the water and watching the world turn upside down. The bend we were on was shallow and there happened to be a safety marshal on the corner, so we simply fell out, stood up right away, dragged the boat to the bank and emptied it out with the help of the marshal (I didn't tell him that he was tipping out my wee). We were back on the river within five minutes of falling in, feeling ever so refreshed on a hot day after the dip.

By the time we entered into the final 10 miles of the kayak section, I decided that I definitely couldn't feel my arms any more. But that was okay, because I could look down and see that they were still moving with the paddles attached to them. And, as the river stretched out again into braided channels, we had officially rediscovered our mojo. I felt relieved to be out of the grip of the gorge and, as the water became shallow once more, we found the energy to burst into an adapted rendition of Lady Gaga's hit 'Shallow'.

'In the sha-la-la-lows! We're right in the shallows now. Where is the deep end? So we can kay-ak, we're stuck in the shallows now…'

At long last, after five hours on the Waimakariri, we rounded the bend to see the Gorge Bridge and the banks below it lined with supporters. The closer we got, the more we could hear their cheers. It was pure magic. We had survived the kayak and, not only that, I had loved every bum-shuffling, rock-dodging, wave-train-jiggling moment of it! The cheers from our support team spurred us on and, after inhaling a final round of energy drinks and raspberry chocco-log goodness, we hopped back on the bikes to take on the last 45 miles.

The temperature was now pushing a toasty 30°C so we

gulped down mouthfuls of water as often as we could, between lungfuls of hot air. We joined another competitor to form a neat little trio train of cyclists for the first 12 miles, and then – Choo! Choo! – up came a group of faster riders behind us. Hallelujah! We hopped right aboard that bullet bike train and managed to cling onto it, tucked in out of the wind as we steamed along the longest, straightest road in New Zealand, all the way to the outskirts of Christchurch.

The final 10 miles through the city were ones of gritted teeth and sore bums, as we battled through a stonking headwind to make progress, but eventually the beach at New Brighton came into view. Our bikes were thrown at random marshals in orange safety jackets and I welcomed the feel of sand beneath my feet for the first time since leaving the Tasman Sea on the west coast.

Entering the finish-line chute felt surreal. The atmosphere was electric. Hordes of people lined the beach, friends and strangers, cheering and clapping, celebratory beers in hands, flags and banners waving. And yet, as things moved in slow motion over those final few sandy yards, nothing mattered beyond Hollie and me. What a rockin' journey it had been. From agreeing to enter the race a year earlier to having crossed New Zealand under human power with a good friend, it had been brutal, beautiful, adrenaline-fuelled and serene all at once. There had been mistakes and disasters and pain aplenty. And I would do it all again in a heartbeat.

As Hollie and I walked, beers in hand, to dip our feet

in the Pacific Ocean, we got word that we'd need to report to prize-giving the following day. The timing chip swap had worked a charm and we'd managed to snatch third place in the tandem team competition – oh how my mum would be delighted. I was still embarrassed by my rookie error on day one but with each post-race beer I sank, it seemed to matter less. We will always wish we had done 'better' and 'differently', after all. But if Coast to Coast had taught me one thing, it's this: when you're surrounded by good people (and armed with an emergency banana), it's never too late to create magic from your mistakes.

Lights Out

(Also known as the afterword)

Well, adventurers – here we are. At the end of my stories, but perhaps just at the beginning of yours?

At the time of finishing this book, we had been in and out of some form of lockdown in the UK for a full year. As the pandemic slips into the rear-view mirror and we motor on through life, I still hope that these pages offered you some escape. I certainly enjoyed the trip down Memory Lane. Not only because nostalgia feels like a snuggly blanket (I could spend hours wrapped up in its warmth), but also because reflecting on these adventures led me to reflect on life as a whole. And alongside the whens and whats of any journey, there will always be the memory of who we believed we were at that point in time or where we believed we were headed – literally and metaphorically. It's a wonder to look back and marvel at our endless capacity for change and for growth.

The year 2020 was certainly a year for both of those things for me and, in the time it took to write this book, I experienced great losses, but there were great gains too. I bought my first house with my lover-lover (one Mr Jamie McDonald), won a literary award (handed to me by Strictly Come

Dancing's Claudia 'The Fringe' Winkleman – OMG) and, most importantly… I gave birth to our first child. I popped her out at home, right next to the Christmas tree and we called her Storm. Ten minutes after she made her debut, thunder and lightning appeared above us in Gloucester – it was all kinds of magical. I dedicated this book to her because I hope that one day, she'll read it and think that her mumma was a cool cat.

All in all, the past year turned out to be nothing like I expected. But, as you'll have noticed, this is true of any adventure. Actually, things going tits-up is the mark of a great adventure. Tell me a story about 'the time it all went right' and I'll get bored halfway through. So why we always expect the greatest adventure of all – life – to go to plan is beyond me.

That's not to say that I didn't cringe at my naivety when putting these stories down on paper. Goodness knows I could have avoided some disasters had I been wiser (like trying to drive through a blizzard), but I have to give that naivety the credit it deserves. Because Naivety gets you out the door. Along with its best bud, Excitement, it goes skipping off down the lane, into the sunset, hoping for the best. It doesn't have time to get side-tracked by the gang from down the street – the Ifs, the Buts and the Maybes. And for that, I'm grateful.

So all that's left to say is: thank you. Thank you for being the inspiration for committing these tales to ink. It's tied a neat little bow around a topsy-turvy time. You've joined me in gallivanting across the globe – we've slept on mountain tops, seen shooting stars, munched on Michelin-starred grub and crunched through the snowy Canadian wilderness. And I'd say, after all of that, you've earned yourself a nice long schnooze. But when you wake, I hope the first thing you do is throw some gubbins in a bag, make a loose plan (or not) and head out the door. Because ultimately life, no matter how chaotic, should be all about two simple things: we should either be at home reading stories or we should be out in the world, creating them.

Happy adventuring,

Anna
x

AUTHOR NOTE

Congratulations, adventuresome human, you have reached the end! A hearty thank you for taking the time to journey around the world with me. I would consider you more magical than my light-up desert DISCO VEST, if you could head over to Amazon or Good Reads right this very moment and leave a review for the book.

Even if it's just a one sentence comment, your words make a massive difference. Reviews are a huge boost to independently published authors, like me, who don't have big publishing houses to spread the word for us. It's safe to say that the more reviews up there, the more likely it is that this book will land in other people's laps.

After then, here's some ways to stay in touch:

Join my mailing list:

AnnaMcNuff.com/McNewsletter

(No Spam, just awesomeness – that's a pinky promise)

If social media is more your kind of fandango, you can say hello here:

On Facebook: **'Anna McNuff'**

On Instagram or Twitter: **@annamcnuff**

Or if social media is your idea of hell, I can also be found here:

AnnaMcNuff.com

hello@annamcnuff.com

Failing that, send me a pigeon.

THANK YOUS

I am always amazed at how many people it takes to put a book into the world and this wodge of words was no exception. Thank you to The Debbatron, aka Debbie Chapman, for being the sensible half of my brain. I'm glad that, through the editing process, we could learn that we both used to attend the ice disco at Guildford Spectrum on a Friday night. Thank you to Sophie Martin for your wisdom in the copy-edit. Despite having just had a baby, you somehow made time to fact check my ramblings and correct my blunders. I will very much miss our email exchanges, comparing notes about Storm's and Issacs's poo issues. And no book would be complete without a final look-over by my awesome Great Aunt Ann – who teaches me that 'less is more' every single time. Any mistakes still left in the text after that team of editorial ninjas are because I've made up my own rules about grammar.

HUGE thankings to Cai Burton for the illustration on the cover. You are so very talented and I am so very glad that my hours of trawling Instagram, looking for artists, led me to your door. I have never created a book that I wanted to stare at for so long. You absolutely nailed the brief and brought everything to life.

A giant thanks to Kim and Sally at Off Grid for putting together yet another slick looking book, making the outside and inside look trés marvellous. I always enjoy working with you, and the opportunity for some hardback cover #FlapChat.

Thank YOU. Those of you who tuned into the adventure bedtime storytelling sessions, follow me on social media, keep tabs via my newsletter or come to watch me run around on stage and tell stories. This book was very much for you, and because of you.

Last, but not least – thank you to my lover-lover Jamie for being a beacon of calm when I panicked that I hadn't finished the bedtime story, EVERY Thursday, an hour before I was due to read it live online. We survived lockdown in a tiny damp flat together, when we're used to the open road. Now that's love. And, of course, thank you to Storm, for doing 'good sleeps' and creating small pockets of peace so that I could get this book finished. You are a cheeky monkey and I love you dearly.

ANNA MCNUFF: KEYNOTE SPEAKER

Anna has delivered motivational, inspiring and entertaining talks for schools, charities and businesses around the world.

'Anna's ability to instill a sense of self-belief in those watching her speak is second to none. Honest, relatable and wonderfully down to earth."

SKY TV

"An incredibly talented speaker. Full of guts, determination, stamina and vision."

BARCLAYS BANK

"Absolutely Fantastic!"

HRH PRINCE EDWARD

"Hugely entertaining with plenty of food for thought."

GlaxoSmithKline

"Without a doubt the most energetic speaker we have ever had. Thank you for helping our team find the courage to face challenges head on."

MARS

"Anna's inspiring stories made the audience really think differently about their own personal and professional challenges."

SKODA

"What a legend! Have you considered a career in stand-up comedy?"

THE NORTH FACE

For more information about booking Anna to speak:

Go to: **annamcnuff.com/speaking**

Or email **speaking@annamcnuff.com**

ALSO BY ANNA MCNUFF

WINNER of the 2020 Amazon Kindle Storyteller Literary Award

"Llama Drama is simply hilarious. If anyone wants something witty and moving at the same time. Also, something empowering, then this is the one for them. I literally inhaled it."

- **Claudia Winkleman**, **TV Presenter and Author**

Armed with a limited grasp of Spanish and determined to meet as many llamas as possible, Anna and her friend Faye set off on a 6-month journey along the spine of the largest mountain range in the world – the Andes.

ALSO BY ANNA MCNUFF

Anna was never anything like those 'real' runners on telly – all spindly limbs, tiny shorts and split times – but when she read about New Zealand's 3,000-kilometre-long Te Araroa Trail, she began to wonder... perhaps being a 'real' runner was over-rated. Maybe she could just run it anyway?

For anyone who has ever dreamt of taking on a great challenge, but felt too afraid to begin – this story is for you.

ALSO BY ANNA MCNUFF

With no previous experience as a long-distance cyclist, Anna decides to clamber atop a beautiful pink bicycle (named Boudica) and set out on an 11,000-mile journey on her own, through each and every state of the USA.

Dodging floods, blizzards and electrical storms, she pedals side by side with mustangs of the Wild West, through towering redwood forests, past the snow-capped peaks of the Rocky Mountains and on to the volcanos of Hawaii.

A stunning tale of self-discovery, told through the eyes of a woman who couldn't help but wonder if there was more to life, and more to America too.

ALSO BY ANNA MCNUFF

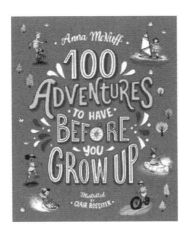

Discover an adventurous life with this energetic guide packed with 100 ideas, big and small.

From building a secret den, to going on a trail run, stargazing in your back garden, visiting a lighthouse and telling midnight ghost stories, every adventure in these pages will get you fired up think creatively and get exploring. No matter where you live or who you are, this book will encourage everyone to fly by the seat of their adventure pants!

ABOUT THE AUTHOR

Anna McNuff is an adventurer, speaker, award-winning author and self-confessed mischief maker. Named by The Guardian as one of the top female adventurers of our time, she is the UK ambassador for Girlguiding, and has run, swum and cycled over 20,000 miles across the globe.

She is best known for her most recent adventure, in which she set off to run 2,620 miles (100 marathons) through Great Britain… in bare feet. Other major journeys include cycling a beautiful pink bicycle through each and every state of the USA, cycling the spine of the Andes and running the length of New Zealand,

When not off adventuring, Anna can be found curled up with a flat white at a local coffee shop in her home city of Gloucester.

Printed in Great Britain
by Amazon

74519519R00116